CREATE
THE
WORK
YOU
WANT

6 STEPS TO CRUSH THE LAUNCH OF YOUR SOLO CONSULTING & PROFESSIONAL SERVICES BUSINESS TODAY

Patricia Steele Ph.D.

Paperback ISBN: 978-1-7330620-0-8
E-book ISBN: 978-1-7330620-1-5

I'd love to hear from you and provide you with some free resources on my website.

www.createtheworkyouwant.com

Come on over to the site and you can download some free stuff, including—

- A handy workbook to help you take notes and sketch out some of your strategy as you read; and
- Some great resources for a low-budget launch, including— sample invoices, budget templates, client contact and time tracking templates.

Thanks so much for reading my book. I truly hope that it is beneficial to you in some significant ways. I can't wait to hear about the work you create!

For my daughters, Abby & Ella, with all my love.
I hope that you find overflowing inspiration to create
your paths one day. Daily you inspire mine.

Table of Contents

Working for Yourself— the Better Path?

Millions of people contemplate creating a business of their own. If you're one of us, thinking about this path, or have already chosen it, you're in good company. We are a group of people driven by the appeal of freedom and greener pastures where we can make our own hours, decide on work intensity, take time off as we see fit, and have more control over our lives. Yet most people never get beyond the uncertainty of starting their own business to take the leap. The fear of the unknown stops them in their tracks. Questions block the way:

- *Could I earn enough money working for myself?*
- *Can I be successful as a solo-entrepreneur?*
- *Do I have what it takes to run my own business?*
- *Is my personality suited to being self-employed?*

I've heard these questions come out of the mouths of amazingly intelligent and successful individuals early, mid and late career—professionals with so much experience and capability that I'm stunned by how fear has stifled their ability to imagine this path.

After 10 years of working for myself and driving the agenda for my work and my life, I can attest to the fact that you *can* start this enterprise—you just need to know the right steps to take to succeed. I've been able to build a successful small business, one that has grown steadily year after year, where I can pay my own salary, hire contractors to work with me, and enjoy my work. This business has helped me to live the kind of life that I want, where I decide the terms: what I want to do, who I work with, when I want to work, and where I want to be. Its growth has no limit: I can hire more and grow more or move on and do something else.

If you are considering your own business or have already launched it, this book will provide you with simple, straightforward, and practical help on everything from finding clients to negotiating contracts and getting paid. These basic points will shape, and perhaps even change, the way you think about your ability to successfully navigate this road. What are you waiting for? Dig in—all the tools you need to create the work you want, and ultimately the life you want, are here waiting for you.

Leslie's Story

After seven years working as an employee in the e-learning industry, Leslie wondered about the potential of working for herself. As a trial run, she took on her own client as a side hustle. Her master's degree in education with a focus on e-learning and design, along with her experience, made her an asset to this client and to others as well. After several years of attracting clients and building her savings, she wondered, "Is now the time to leave my W-2 behind and start working for myself full-time?"

Leslie's question is one that many of us ask. My own journey to self-employment began almost 10 years ago, and it has been a process of trial and error. But since taking that step, I have found tremendous joy in sharing this path with others and offering advice as they consider a similar course. Today, I'm passionate about encouraging others to choose this path of self-employment. It is not only possible to step into this way of life; for many of us, it's a better way to live. As I've spoken with people of various ages, educational levels, training, and experience, I've witnessed a force that pulls them toward their own venture.

I wrote this book not to convince people that they should choose this path but, instead, to clear away some of the brush on the trail that feeds the fear of what's ahead. The brush includes the practical questions of how to get started, what to charge, how to keep a steady flow of customers, where to work, and which strategies are most likely to keep you connected and productive. My hope is that this book will address your concrete questions and help you tune into the voice inviting you to the path of working for yourself.

The Certainty of Job Insecurity

I would bet that the majority of the people you know find a deep sense of security in their W-2 income and bi-weekly paycheck, possibly accompanied by employer-provided health insurance and matching 401K benefits if they're lucky. As a 46-year-old, post-divorce mom raising two children, I can understand why most people view the traditional employment path as the safest route to a secure future. But the notion that any employment path we choose will be a sure thing is simply a false sense of security. Uncertainty is *everywhere* around us.

Few people work in the same job for their entire careers. According to the Bureau of Labor Statistics, wage and salary workers stay with their employer on average about four years.[1] Whereas some people might switch jobs every few years but stay in the same industry, the skills that once sufficiently equipped them for a particular career require refining and updating far more frequently in this technological era. Even the most commonly cited jobs that were once considered reliable (i.e. guaranteed pension-for-life employment) are slowly disappearing and no longer a solid bet.

Jobs that seem permanent are no longer permanent. I've seen friends go into depressive slumps that lasted for months or years after being terminated or laid off by an employer or losing a job after a company merger or transition. The sense of security that comes with someone else issuing your paycheck each month disintegrates when that rug is pulled out from underneath you. Add that stress to the assault on one's identity and sense of self that often comes with losing a job, and you have a situation that can be truly destructive.

Even as I write this manuscript in early 2019, the federal workforce is in the midst of the longest furlough it has ever experienced. Federal workers have no idea how long they will go without a paycheck. In my metro area of Washington, D.C., city councilmembers are arranging relief for rent, utilities, and food scarcity because federal pay periods have already been missed

---

[1] "Employee Tenure Summary," U.S. Bureau of Labor Statistics, September 20, 2018, https://www.bls.gov/news.release/tenure.nr0.htm.

and no one knows when checks will be issued. This crisis won't go on forever, but it's an excellent incentive to rethink one's sense of financial security.

Changing Tide of Employment

You might be surprised at how many people are now working for themselves. Workers who are self-employed, work for someone who is self-employed, or have a side job (a.k.a. a "gig" or "side hustle") make up a significant portion of the American workforce. They span a range of industries and cite a range of motivations for choosing work scenarios that are an alternative to the traditional full-time, single-company job.

While the self-employed represent 1 in 10 American workers, their reach extends deep into the national workforce. A full 30% of the U.S. workforce is comprised of self-employed individuals and the workers they hire.[2] In fact, most businesses in the U.S.— nearly 80%—are considered "microbusinesses," defined as those with fewer than 10 employees; and 9 out of 10 have fewer than 20 employees.[3] The self-employed and those they employ comprise a critical majority of three industries: agriculture, forestry and fishing (81%); construction (68%); and professional and business services (53%).[4]

---

[2] Pew Research Center, "Three-in-Ten U.S. Jobs Are Held by the Self-Employed and the Workers They Hire,"
http://www.pewsocialtrends.org/2015/10/22/three-in-ten-u-s-jobs-are-held-by-the-self-employed-and-the-workers-they-hire/
[3] OECD, "Entrepreneurship at a Glance: 2018 Highlights,"
http://www.oecd.org/sdd/business-stats/EAG-2018-Highlights.pdf
[4] Pew Research Center, "Three-in-Ten..."

American workers with side jobs total nearly 4 in 10 (37%) of the national workforce, and they make an average of $8,000 annually. Overall, workers with side jobs are more likely to be members of the Millennial generation[5] than any other, and the likelihood of having a side job declines with older generations.[6]

No single job function or industry dominates the side hustle economy. The most popular side hustle is home repair and landscaping, but they account for only 12% of all side hustles. Behind home repair and landscaping, the most common side hustles are online sales (7%), crafts (7%), and childcare (6%).[7]

Living the Life You Choose

Security is not the only reason people set their path on particular careers. We may choose our careers because we love the work, or because we could tolerate the work in exchange for a certain salary and lifestyle. But this love for our career can change and evolve. I'm sure that you can conjure the image of friends and family members who launched careers they once loved but suffer in misery with work they no longer enjoy, co-workers they don't like, or bosses they don't respect. In the midst of these careers they

---

[5] It's important to keep in mind that Millennials are set to surpass Baby Boomers as the nation's largest generation in 2019. (Pew Research Center, "Millennials projected to overtake Baby Boomers as America's largest generation," http://www.pewresearch.org/fact-tank/2018/03/01/millennials-overtake-baby-boomers/

[6] Bankrate, "The average side hustler earns over $8K annually," https://www.bankrate.com/personal-finance/smart-money/side-hustles-survey-june-2018/

[7] Ibid.

feel trapped—they see no means to escape. Or maybe they just want to ride out the years to retirement or the promised "security" of a pension but quietly resent each day. Often something happens to push us out of our comfort zones and onto new paths.

Bob's Story

Bob was a banker all his life, having started at a notable Wall Street bank in 1958 while just a teenager. He stayed with that company through his military service, rising up through the ranks while earning college degrees, for a total of 37 years. This job offered everything a person needed— excellent work opportunities and room for advancement, health benefits, on-site doctors for regular checkups, free lunches in the employee cafeteria, life insurance options, and even a pension.

Then one day, after close to four decades of faithful service and on the brink of closing a major sale for the company that would have provided one of the largest bonuses of his career, Bob's division and the entire trust service team of about 900 people were sold. Almost all of the team members were transferred to the new bank where they would continue providing trust services for the clients acquired in the sale. But left standing in the cold was the roughly 12-person sales team, which included Bob, whose positions were now eliminated. To say that he was stunned would be an understatement. He was 55 years old, far from his desired retirement age, with more uncertainty than anything else. He had no choice but to reinvent himself. Should he consider starting his own business?

As Bob's situation demonstrates, life has no guarantees or promise of another day. I realize that most of us are not making decisions solely for ourselves—we have family members to take care of and financial obligations to meet. I'm not suggesting that we abandon those responsibilities as we search for greater job and life satisfaction. But I do want to present a challenge to your thinking: You are responsible for creating the life that you live, and my hope is that this book makes another path possible besides staying in a job that does not bring you joy. I've tried to make the guidance in these pages simple so that you can identify a new course, perhaps as a side hustle, your next professional path, or maybe even a brand new multi-million-dollar business. My goal is to illuminate a path and help you envision your own business. You *can* choose a different path for yourself—one where you create the work life you desire, make the money you want, and choose the team you like for the journey.

Leslie and Bob—Creating Their Own Paths

Just 11 years into her career as an instructional designer for e-learning, Leslie stepped away from her role as an employee and started working for herself. She wanted the flexibility that came from freelancing—like the ability to pick up her daughter from school.

This was not an easy move for Leslie: "It's certainly a lot easier to just keep your seat in the corporate career path. But I love the challenge ... the endless creativity that is required [to run your own business is fantastic]. It's never the same thing, and you're constantly growing and learning. I love this job. It's the greatest job in the world."

Bob was laid off from his company in a merger, but he was not laid off empty-handed. Having worked in the trust banking industry for so many years, Bob had a litany of skills. He had spent 20 years in trust operations and served as sales manager of custody services sold to banks, insurance companies, and foundations in the major regions of the U.S. He was also a master at networking, so respected that the outplacement services firm hired by the bank for outgoing executives invited him to teach the course on sales networking for their other clients. Even so, Bob figured out quickly that he needed to hone other skills too. Having relied heavily on administrative support, he did not yet know how to do basic keyboarding, use word processing programs, or have any other computer skills, for that matter. So Bob went out and obtained the skills updating and training he required.

After a short stint with one more employer, he launched TRP Consulting. (The initials stand for the first letter of each of his children's names: Theresa, Robert, and Patricia. Yes, "Bob" is my father!) Not only did he become the ultimate professional services consultant from that point to his retirement, but the firm which had acquired his company engaged him as a consultant a few years later.

This Book is For You

If you are reading this introductory chapter, then you're somewhere on the path of considering self-employment. People start their journeys to working for themselves in different ways. No single path exists.

This book is for you, no matter where you're starting. If you're later in your career, seasoned with experience and ready to launch your own company working directly with clients, you will find a wealth of resources in these pages. If you're early in your career with less experience, wanting to test the waters of working for yourself, freelancing, or maybe just developing a side business, these chapters offer plentiful guidance for you too. And if you're uniquely skilled in an area of clear demand, and you're *just ready* to launch a business in which you call the shots, build the teams, and choose the clients, much here can benefit you as well. Even if you're already self-employed, you can discover pointers and assurance about how to move forward.

The idea for this book arose from the endless number of conversations that I've had over the years with others who have pondered the choice of working for themselves. Some have concluded that it's not for them, but more are inclined toward the idea but have a great deal of uncertainty. That latter group is the main audience for each chapter of guidance.

This material is targeting those in professional service businesses—providing a service to other businesses. I've worked with and talked with individuals working in a variety of industries as I wrote this book: researchers, policy experts, evaluators, data analytics consultants, instructional designers, marketing and communications professionals, bookkeepers, architects, financial investors, human resource consultants, organization development coaches, student financial aid experts, meeting planners and facilitators, executive coaches, strategy consultants, and more.

People working in these arenas—and many others—will find the chapters that follow useful for growing their businesses.

A Guidebook for Your Trip

The next chapter is designed to simplify your business launch into six straightforward steps. Read that chapter in full—while taking notes and brainstorming your action steps—then set the book down. Once you've had a chance to make some progress on those first steps, come back and read the remaining chapters. Chapters Three to Eight dig into each of the six steps, so if you've got a step down and done, skip onto the next one. The final chapters offer parting words and advice on being *excellent* in your new business.

Thank you for reading. I wish you well discovering how to turn your best asset—you—into the future business you want.

Six Steps to Creating Your New Business

Right now, in your head, consider what it will take to launch your business. Make a mental list. What do you imagine that you need to create and do? Perhaps you feel that you need to have a name, establish a formal entity, get a business bank account, talk to an accountant or a lawyer, create a fancy website, print business cards, get some letterhead with your logo, and write a business plan. Well, I'm here to tell you, this isn't true! You can declare *today* as the day you established your business.

Now, brace yourself. With the next statement, I'm going out on a limb. Here it is: The biggest thing standing between you and the new business you want to create is *you*. This may seem like an outrageous concept—but whether you're currently employed, in between employment, or professionally retired, the first step toward starting your business is choosing this path. It doesn't matter whether you'll continue working a full-time job with a side hustle for a while; or if you'll obtain funds from a company, investor, friend, or your family; or if you will pour coffee at Starbucks while you figure it all out. The only thing standing between you and your self-employment is a choice.

Choosing to Start on This Path

The day you choose to do this, a new pathway for your life begins. I know, you're thinking, "But how is it that I'm in business when I don't have any clients or customers paying me yet?" This is where I want you to just accept the uncertainty and be confident in yourself when I tell you this truth: Finding clients is not the hard part. Deciding to choose this path is the real challenge.

We are often afraid to declare a direction or intention without someone presenting it to us for consideration or without a team of friends and family assuring us it's the right path for us. But this is a path you have to create yourself. You already have everything that you need, even though you may need some guidance or instruction on how to proceed. This path is not about a cookie-cutter route—it's about using your resources, intellect, creativity, drive and motivation, inspiration, and skills and experience. You get to create the path—and ultimately the life—that you want to lead. Just say it to yourself, "I am launching my business today."

Here are the three main reasons that people will hire you: They like you, they respect you, and they trust you. Yes, of course your skills and your experience are a big part of what you have to offer in business and are important drivers in the respect category. But all the experience, training, and degrees in the world will not help you land a job or a contract if people do not like working with you, do not respect the work quality you've provided in the past, or do not trust you to deliver what you say you'll deliver.

People who know me have heard me highlight these big three before—like, respect, and trust. These are the key drivers for getting your first contract and getting referrals to future contracts. Let's flesh out these characteristics:

- **You must be able to work with people.** The world is a big place with many different types of people, but we tend to work with those we like. You don't have to be everything to everyone, but you need to have a flexible personality that can interact in healthy ways with a variety of people. You must be slow to get annoyed and think before you speak or type. You're not trying to work with the whole world—just those who need the services you offer.
- **You must have demonstrated capabilities of some kind.** You don't need to have every skill—just one skill and some history of clear capability in that area where people respect your work. It helps to have "witnesses" who can attest to your competence. The other skills that you need can be learned along the way, or you can hire others to help you.
- **You must be someone who follows through with commitments.** Most business arrangements are based on trust, so people must know that you are the kind of person who will show up on time, deliver on time, and provide a high-quality product in all scenarios. In other words, you must be a person of integrity.

If these three statements are true about you, you are in a position to run a successful professional service business. What is required next is your focused attention and hard work to make your business goals a reality.

In his excellent book, *Atomic Habits*, writer and entrepreneur James Clear differentiates between getting started on something new versus just planning to do something new. He notes that at times, "we are so focused on figuring out the best approach that we never get around to taking action." And while I want you to read my book and digest all of its good advice, I don't want you to wait one day before launching into action. Follow along with me in this overview chapter where I will quickly walk you through the six steps to launching your business.

My intention is to make this process as simple as possible. For some of you, this six-step list could be done in a single day or weekend. There is nothing standing in your way and you're ready to do this thing. For others, this six-step process will take some time and contemplation; you're not going to dive deep until you've got something really secure. Either way, the steps are the same.

Step 1: Define One Core Business Service

To start, you must consider at least one service that you can provide to clients based on the skills that you have—something that you could make available to clients *today* that you know is in demand. You don't need to know everything that your company will one day be on the day you launch your business; you just have to know one service that you can offer to address a problem that exists. For me when I started out, helping organizations use data was my one thing. I had no idea all the paths my company would take me down over the next decade, but data utilization was where I started, and it was surely enough because many organizations needed help building their data capacity.

So what is your one thing? Start looking over your past work and consider the skills you offer. What do you do best? What do other people say you do well? For many of you reading this book, this part is easy. You know exactly where your sweet spot is and you've trained professionally to do it. But I want to push you further. Forget about your training and consider what it is that gets you excited and impassioned. That activity usually indicates some kind of symmetry between what you're doing and what you're good at—a positive alignment of skills and preferences. Try to articulate some of those.

Early on in my business, when defining my skill sets, I knew that I was good at using data, analyzing data, and helping others think creatively about how to use data. I had expertise utilizing a number of national government- and nongovernment-provided data sets to answer questions about higher education problems. What I did not realize at the time is that I'm also incredibly resourceful and can figure out solutions to almost any problem. I'm a skilled strategist, and clients enjoy talking through ideas, problems, and solutions with me. I'm also an excellent connector. I love making pertinent connections between people for my clients' benefit. And I'm trustworthy: I follow through on projects, so even if a project is not in my direct expertise, clients want to hire me because they trust that I'll get a job done well. What's on your list? (Yes, write it down, now.)

Once you've nailed down the skill set that you want to offer and defined that core business, share it with the world. As you're just starting out, a simple, updated LinkedIn page is sufficient. You can highlight your skills and what you intend to provide as a business.

If you have some extra time, you can also create a website from a simple template. You don't need extensive information, but just an online business card presence. You can revise and revisit your visual communications and digital strategies once your business is up and running, so keep on moving to the next step.

Step 2: Identify Your Clients and Customers

Of course, your customer base starts with contacts you already have. Make a list of all the people you know personally or professionally who intersect even marginally with the business services you're interested in providing. Divide the list into these columns:

- Companies/organizations that could directly benefit from my knowledge/services
- People/companies whom you know at listed companies/organizations
- People/companies whom you know that could refer you to contacts at listed companies/organizations
- People you like and who might offer you good advice about launching your own professional services business

Get elaborate here. If lists don't help you think creatively, you can instead create a mind map of the companies with lines showing relationships between people you know and the various companies/organizations.

Attracting customers depends so much on how you describe your services. At many points in my career, I've done what any good consultant has done: I looked at what other people do. This is not stealing—it's benchmarking. You want to see examples of existing companies offering services like the ones that you're interested in selling. Turn to your trusted friend, Google, and start exploring companies big and small that seem noteworthy to you. It will amaze you to see what other people offer and how they describe it. Craft your own language that aligns with your vision of the services you can offer. Keep in mind that this is something that will evolve over time and therefore does not need to be perfect as you're starting out. You will walk away from this exercise feeling assured that you have something worth promoting.

Step 3: Connect With Your People to Explore Opportunities

It's time to begin meeting with your core contacts. Start scheduling time to talk with people in person or by phone. Relationships are the main way that you're going to launch your business, so you have to actually tell people what you're planning to do. Reach out via email to your key people to lay the groundwork for your conversations.

With someone I'm not personal friends with, I might say something like the following over the phone:

Thanks for taking the time to talk with me. I wanted to tell you a little bit about what I've been up to and what I'm thinking of doing in the next couple years. I'm launching a [professional services/consulting/solutions] business because I've realized that

I'm really passionate about working with organizations around [the thing you love to work on]. My different roles have given me experience in this arena, but now I'm interested in working directly with [business/organizational/government] leaders on a [contract/project] basis. So, what do you think? ... PAUSE

Give folks a moment to respond with their thoughts and ideas. If they have nothing to say besides, "it sounds good," you can follow up with some questions:

- *Where do you see a need for these kinds of services? Or, to what extent do you see a need for these kinds of services?*
- *Does your company/organization have a need for services like this? What other service needs does your company have?*
- *Do you have any suggestions or advice for me as I establish some ongoing contract work in this arena?*
- *I have calls/meetings set up with X, Y and Z—have you worked with them or do you know them?*
- *Can you suggest other people or organizations that I should talk to about the work I'm trying to do?*

Then, it's time to follow through on every suggestion provided to you by a core contact. It is 100% necessary that you follow up with any and every lead that comes your way in any conversation. If you meet someone at an event or have a phone call, follow up with a written message, reminding them of your meeting and thanking them for their time. If you bump into someone and you discuss a project they're working on, follow up by asking for more information, and actually read it and respond. You engage by showing genuine interest. You can also connect with folks that you meet via LinkedIn and by following them on Twitter (if they're tweeters).

Being genuine and showing interest is key. If someone mentions a contact or a potential project to discuss and you don't follow up, you look like a slacker, especially if someone has gone out of their way to make an introduction for you. Every interaction with a potential client or a person who might introduce you to a client is an opportunity to demonstrate that you are a person who can be trusted. You are a person who follows through. You are a person that they should hire if they want to get things done.

Step 4: Plan How and Where You Will Work

Determine where you're doing business. Changing addresses for your business can be a true administrative burden and an expense, so it's important to get this right. Each time I've changed addresses, it meant updating registries, changing addresses with clients, fixing my website, re-doing my business cards, and so forth.

It's important to note that some states and counties have restrictions on whether you can do business from your home or have forms and requirements to fill. Before you opt to make your business address your home, research this with your state or county business services agencies and offices. You can look on your state business registration website and determine if the information resides there. If not, you can call the business centers in your state and get information over the phone (though try to verify this information in writing somewhere). This is not the time to get buried in the complexities of state income and corporate taxes to determine which state is a better fit for you. This is the time to launch your business, and to do this, you need a mailing address, period.

If I were starting out today, I would have obtained a P.O. Box for my business and maintained it for the life of my company. Over the course of my 10 years in business I've had three different offices spaces and four different homes; paying the small fee for a professional address is worthwhile. Today, a number of co-location spaces offer mail services for a fee as well.

Step 5: Determine What You Can Charge

The first question that most people encounter when they launch their business is: what do I charge? It's a big question, but it's also fairly straightforward. Depending on who your first prospective client is and how well you know them, it may be possible to have a frank conversation about what is their norm and what are they comfortable paying in these kinds of contractual relationships. If that first client is not a close colleague, then you'll need to do some investigative work. Think about other consultants you know and reach out for a chat. Or if you know people in hiring positions or management positions at various companies, ask them to give you a sense of what they pay to contractors of different kinds. You'll need to seek input from those on the for-profit, nonprofit, and government side if you are working in any of these spaces.

The worst-case scenario is that you mention your daily rates to a prospective client and you're way out of their ballpark. It's okay to say that you're still determining your rates. For example,

"I'm charging X per day for X services, but I'm eager to make it work with you, so I do want to be flexible." Say it clearly and look the person in the eye. You don't need to apologize for wanting to be paid a fair wage. You're self-employed now, and no one is contributing to your 401K, paying for your vacations, or paying your taxes or insurance costs. Most seasoned professionals understand this situation, so the higher-than-usual-rates charged by consultants is expected. Here is the key thing: When you are meeting with clients, you don't have to focus on your rates. Instead, focus on their needs. If you can convey that you understand those needs, then the price won't matter because they will be ready to hire you to get the job done.

Step 6: Make Simple Plans for Managing Money and Contracts

As you launch your new business, you'll want simple plans in place for managing money and contracts. Later, I'll discuss in greater length different approaches to invoicing and managing money, but for now you need a plan that you can implement if your first client(s) called you to start working next week. Many banks will charge higher fees for business banking accounts, so for this initial period, simply open a separate checking or savings account within your current personal banking space. I've always liked having my business banking and personal banking in the same space for ease of transferring money. Later on, you can explore which banks offer the best business account options, but for this interim period, any separate personal account will do.

Once that account is established, you can deposit all funds into that account. If you put a few hundred dollars in when you open the account, you can draw all expenses for the business from it for easy tracking of revenues and expenses. If you have a credit card available that you can devote exclusively to the business, you could also use that for expenses. The important feature of finances at this stage is keeping the business transactions separate so that you have very clear records. Then once a month you can enter all of this information in a spreadsheet and create the first profit and loss statement of your business. Once you have grown your business, you can hire a bookkeeper or use a business financial software, like QuickBooks or one of its many competitors.

Summary

So, let's recap. Offering professional services consulting can happen at any point in your career as long as you are someone with people skills, proven capacities, and a track record for getting things done. Only six things need to happen to get your show on the road:

Step 1: Define one core business service

Step 2: Identify your clients and customers

Step 3: Connect with your people to explore opportunities

Step 4: Plan how and where you will work

Step 5: Determine what you can charge

Step 6: Make simple plans for managing money and contracts

Can you believe it? You are just six simple steps away from starting your own business, from using what you know to create the work you want. What are you waiting for?

Defining Your Business

Why Are You Launching a Business?

People come to the life plan of self-employment in a number of ways. No single path exists. Some may choose self-employment because other opportunities have dried up. Some are frustrated with the field around them. Others may have a particular set of services that they want to offer—that they know have market value all on their own, without the control of a larger company.

Whatever your reasons, you must have a passion for what you're going to do. You need to care about the work. It is certainly possible to be financially successful and not care one bit about your field, but such success is unlikely. Success emanates from natural and genuine passion. What do you care about at this stage of your life?

When I initially started my business, I was enthusiastic about the role of education in creating greater equity of opportunity in the U.S. This cause originally motivated me, but the ultimate passion I discovered was illuminating, through the use of data, how people could do their work better and smarter. This affection was the trigger that launched my business toward success.

When You're First Starting Out

Ultimately, the process of launching your business is a matter of thinking through what it is that you have to offer. What are you good at? What are you known for? What are you passionate about? What comes easy to you? Where do you already have natural connections? Build on those things.

The harder part is figuring out your *value*. What do you have that people will pay for in the markets where you are seeking contracts? You need to get this part crystal clear, because it will give you the confidence to ask for the money you deserve.

People hire contractors for a variety of reasons. But why would or should an employer hire you as a consultant rather than hire a full-time employee? You must understand that in many cases, having access to a consultant is a tangible benefit for a CEO or company/organization leader. Here are the factors in your favor:

- *Remedy*. Sometimes consultants are an immediate remedy to a problem; for example, an employee is out on leave, or an existing employee is unqualified to do what is needed.
- *Focus*. Often, a consultant is someone who can be 100% focused on a project or a goal for the company while other employees are pulled in 20 different directions. Hiring a consultant is an opportunity for the company/organization to get something done that wouldn't otherwise be done.

- *Expertise.* Consultants can often bring services and skills that are not internally present or where highly specialized services are required. Perhaps an organization wants to do something that is outside of its current business efforts. Or perhaps the company wants an objective, independent party to execute some work. Consultants may be the answer.

- *Flexibility.* When companies bring on consultants, they have the opportunity to expand upon their company for a short period of time in areas they might want to expand permanently. This is a chance for them to try such a venture on for size before committing long-term.

- *Market Gap.* Sometimes consultants can build their business based on gaps in the market. Mike is a perfect example of this niche work. He's an architect by training with a passion for designing walkable communities. Mike's business was built on the intersection of what developers do in real-estate investment and what builders do in creating properties; neither is necessarily thinking about the experience of the residents on the developed property outside of the buildings. Mike created a business out of this gap by creating a needed service—serving as the town architect for the design of walkable communities.

Whatever your reason for launching the business, the first question you need to face is, what are you going to offer? You don't need to know everything, but you need to spend some time thinking through your skills. For some of you, this offering is self-evident—you're a graphic designer or a writer or an analyst. If that's the case, then you just need to get more specific. Do you want to do certain types of design work? Do you want to work with specific types of clients?

Even though I have a whole host of advertised skills, sometimes people still hire me to help them manage things that are somewhat outside of those skills. For example, my firm has had multiple clients acquire our services to manage proposals from other companies. We've also had clients hire us to do strategic planning and meeting management. Meanwhile, our core services are research and evaluation. Are you willing to work outside your box? Try to think broadly.

Move your thinking outside your head—write or type responses to these prompts:

- Make a list of the skills that you have in spades, skills from which others could benefit.
- Make a list of the type of work that you love and feel inspired by when doing it.
- Make a list of professional services that companies and organizations in your field often hire outside people to do.

Once you've made these lists, you may begin to see some overlapping areas, but hopefully what emerges is the first image of what you think your business could be. Try to code the lists then group into categories. For example, do the skills you listed fall into creative services, administrative, strategic support, research, evaluation, content development, or project management? Once you have delineated some categories, you have the makings of your first offerings list.

Mike knew he had urban design skills that had earned him a strong reputation while working for his previous company. But he was hungry for longer-term relationships: he wanted to not only provide initial ideas to developers and municipalities but also to consult with clients through the implementation. By articulating these skills and passions, he envisioned a company of his own.

Now that you've gone through the process of identifying the value you offer and articulating your services, you're ready to narrow your offering down to a few sentences—the elevator pitch. Writing something brief enough and clear enough to convey what you do in the time it takes to ride an elevator will help you to crystalize what it is that you're planning to provide in your consulting business.

Finally, now that you have zeroed in on your core business service, you need to decide whether you want to follow this self-employed path for the long haul (a year or more) or just for a short season (less than a year). If it's the latter, you have no other legal work to do. You're simply going to offer your services as an individual, using your own name and social security number (you can obtain a separate EIN if you like, but it's not needed). You might consider keeping a spreadsheet of all your business expenses so that when it's time to file your taxes, you have a clear log of what you spent for reporting on your Schedule C at tax time. If you are making a longer-term commitment, then you need to ponder whether you want to create an entity (such as an LLC or sole proprietorship) with a name or just name your consultancy after yourself.

Creating a Virtual Presence

As you consider what to call your business, you'll need to look in two places to see if a name can be yours: your state registry and the World Wide Web. Does anyone else in your state have that name? Is a URL available for purchase with the name you want (or some modification of it)?

If you're not ready yet to think about what to call your business (and I recommend that you don't name it yet), then just buy the URL for your name. If you're going to name your entity now, then check the business entity search on your state's website to see if the name is available and confirm that the name is not copyrighted already. You'll find that many common names are already purchased, so you have to get creative. I was quite glad that I gave my company a broad name in the very beginning that made it feasible for it to grow in a number of different directions. Once you have a unique name, then buy the URL. If you're new to business, I would recommend buying your own URL on GoDaddy or some other URL sales site.

You need a virtual presence and a business card, mainly to lead people that you meet in the real world to a place where they can learn more about you. Every time I'm at a major event meeting people or speaking in public or meeting with a client, hits on my LinkedIn profile and my website jump. Online profiles are the main way that people verify something about you or point their colleagues to you.

If you're just starting out, a simple, updated LinkedIn or Facebook business page is sufficient. Look at similar consultants and how they define themselves and their work. Your LinkedIn profile can still be a list of your prior employers, but it needs to also highlight your skills and what you intend to provide as a business. Your lead line should have a one-sentence description of you and your attributes as well as a list of your core services. Then provide a list of previous employment that highlights your skills and assets, not just your job titles.

If you have extra time, you can also create a website from a simple template. You don't need extensive information. This is not the time to worry about mission statements and blog posts. Instead, design a clean opening page that summarizes what services you provide, then a secondary page with an overview of who you are. You can even drop in your resume/C.V. and some references.

Summary

These early moves are some of the most important. Of all the skills you have, determine which set inspires you and offers a value to businesses. Create your elevator pitch, settle on a name, and create a virtual presence. Once these tasks are checked off, you're done with Step #1.

Finding and Keeping Clients

When it comes to officially launching your own business, finding clients is a crucial step. Most people who I speak to about launching their own consultancies say things like "I don't really like selling myself," or "I'm not comfortable with sales." But these people need to shift their mindset: Sales is not about self-promotion; it is all about *relationships*. This aspect of building your business is not primarily about generating sales or websites or marketing brochures or newsletters—it's about your network. You need to think about who is in that network and plan for how to engage them. Your job is not to push yourself onto others; you are not promoting a false product or capability. This part of doing business is all about being yourself—building your business by engaging with the people in your professional and social networks.

Being self-employed as a consultant is surely not for hermits. If you're a particularly gloomy and negative person who prefers to be on your own most of the time, then perhaps your networks are quite small. But most people, whether they are extroverted or introverted by nature, have deep benches of people who really like them, respect them, or both. This is the network on which to start your business.

After running into a wall in the restaurant business, Randi decided to launch *By the Book Consulting*, an accounting and financial advising business. Once she had her business ready to roll, she sent an email to every single person she knew, letting them know about her new venture. In turn, these people with whom she had credibility spread the word, and soon the clients started rolling in.

Take out a piece of paper, or just jot notes in the column of this book. Who is on the list of people who really like you, who know that you're a trustworthy person, and who could attest to your reliability and character? Make a second list of those people who know your work—former bosses, supervisors, colleagues or people who worked for you. Who can attest to your intelligence, creativity, and capabilities? This list is the start of your business. This is the place you will go to seek out work and referrals.

Sometimes networking connections happen in the process of a job search. Individuals reach a point in their careers where they have quite a bit of experience under their belts, and they feel a bit odd to go into a new organization without a more senior title. This is a natural point to begin considering a consulting path, but it is by no means the only one. Perhaps an organization is recruiting you for a full-time position, and in the process, you learn about the work and their needs. You can always offer to work on a per diem basis while they conduct their search for the right person—especially if it's clear that you have skills that the company is seeking.

One mid-career woman that I coached on launching her business had job offers coming her way at the same time. The appeal of the "secure" W2 paycheck was a strong draw for her when no other client projects were lined up. The problem was that the position was in a geographically undesirable place to live. I challenged her thinking a bit—she was far too seasoned and skilled to take a job she didn't want. I asked her to consider using the job offer as an opportunity to negotiate a contract. When she approached the hiring manager with a proposal for addressing the company's immediate needs via a short-term contract, he bit! And right there she nailed her first three-day-a-week contract for a six-month period. Now she has a consistent income as well as plenty of time for business development while she's starting out.

Sometimes finding the first client really is this simple. Just remember that you have value to add; many companies need that value and they need it now. Having that "anchor client" at the start of your business can be a terrific launch pad.

I would caution you about taking on full-time, short-term contracts. As appealing as they may seem at first, those all-consuming projects will get in the way of creating the business and the life you want. Push a client to be precise about what it is that they need. If it's to temporally fill the shoes of a person on leave, negotiate at least a day or two per week away from the job with limited availability to the client. You will need this time to continue growing your business.

Who's on Your Core Client List?

Who are the clients that you want to serve? I almost hate to start out here because I don't want to limit your thinking. When I launched by business, I was sure that I would be working with all the different nonprofits out there in the college access world. But as it turned out, my most significant clients ended up being foundations, think tanks, and professional associations. I still ended up working on college access issues, but those organizations were rarely my paying clients. Even though it may evolve, your core client list should start with the clients you imagine serving.

Of course, this list is tied to the *impact* you hope to make. It's not enough to just want to make money (though that is a perfectly legitimate driving force for your business). What future change do you wish to support as a result of your energy and gifts? Once you've identified that vision, ask, who is at the core of this universe? For my business, I feel a deep personal commitment to improving access to educational opportunity for those who are under-represented in colleges in the U.S. What drives me is that I believe college can be a great equalizing force in society; a college education has the ability to eliminate intergenerational poverty for families. Thus, my core work is focused on any organization that is removing barriers to opportunity. My target organizations that could benefit from my experience are college access nonprofits (see Figure 1). Yet, I learned that my service ecosystem has many others who care about the same outcomes.

Identify your core clients by thinking through the different levels of potential clients who could benefit from your services. Who are your target organizations or companies that could benefit from your expertise? Which companies or entities provide funds or other kinds of support or engagement to those target entities? What are the other related organizations? As you think through each of these levels, consider avenues for engaging with these potential clients.

Figure 1: Identifying Core Clients

Target organizations that could benefit from my expertise	• College access organizations • High schools and related high school-service organizations
Companies/entities that provide funds to target organizations	• Foundations and statewide and local funders • State agencies • Colleges and universities • Professional associations • Government entities that support college access programs • State Department of Education offices
Related engaged organizations	• Chambers of Commerce • Regional associations of higher ed • Higher ed accreditors • Higher ed funders • Education lenders and loan servicers • Department of Labor job centers • Companies with employer-sponsored grants for college

Business Development Through Events

If you live in a major city, you might consider devoting some time in your week to business development events. In other words, get off the computer and into a room with colleagues. At times like these, it's good to have already done some work on the elevator speech and have some business cards handy. If you don't live in a major city, then it's time to figure out what trips you need to book to get face-to-face with important contacts.

The focus of your business development has to shift to places where your potential clients actually spend time. When I was a young professional, I would often go to the association conference in my professional field, which was a wonderful place for me to learn about new things and acquire professional development. However, it offered little potential for me to meet with prospective clients and discuss the business services I offered. Instead, I had to find ways to attend the associations that my desired clients attended. Keep in mind that major annual conferences often get booked far in advance, and agendas and content are fixed. If you want to attend an annual conference that is important to your business, then find a way to attend as a contributor, speaker, volunteer or program reviewer. Each of these paths could make it far less expensive (if not free) to attend.

In my city, Washington, D.C., endless free events take place all the time. Policy groups, advocacy groups, nonprofits, think tanks, and even government entities host programs regularly. I could fill my calendar 100% of the year attending these. The key is to figure out strategic choices for your business. Who are the prospective clients that you want to meet, and where will they be? Once you have figured out these key events and locations, here is what you need to do:

- You actually have to attend the event. Research the people attending and hosting the event prior to going. Show up early, be dressed appropriately for the event, do not sit down and start checking your phone—engage! If your face is buried in your phone, no one will talk to you. Meet the folks organizing the meeting. Sometimes the folks checking people in can be your best asset—you can learn about their work (if they're not too busy), learn who's who in the organization, learn who the speakers are, who typically attends, etc. Now that you've got the lay of the land, you can make some connections around the room.

- Participate in the event by taking notes, asking questions, and connecting with people who make relevant comments when the event is over. Don't check your Facebook page or text with your friends. If there is an opportunity to make a comment or question, use that opportunity to introduce yourself and what you do—that you're a consultant working on X and X.

- Be ready to talk about what you're doing in a genuine way. If you're brand new to consulting, say so. If you're dipping your toe in, be straight about it. "I was recently working on X issues with X, but I'm exploring the feasibility of working per diem so I can focus on the skills I've honed doing X, X, and X."

- Get to know people; ask genuine questions of interest about what they're doing. Make authentic connections. When there's not a natural connection, you can just simply be curious. You never know when a relationship or connection can lead to future business, even if the initial conversation is marginally related to your interest. Once someone has your card and knows what you're doing, the next time their friends says, "Our company is backlogged—we could really use some consulting help for...," the person you just met knows someone—you! This is the definition of business networking.

- After you have met someone, follow up with a note via email. If you have an interest in continued conversation, schedule a coffee to talk further. You don't need to say two words in that coffee conversation about wanting their business or selling yourself. You just need to be genuinely yourself—right where you are. They can see your LinkedIn profile; you don't need to give them a rundown of where you studied, who you know, or what your five previous jobs were. You just need to get to know their work and let them know the work you want. Period. Trust me on this point. No one wants to hire someone who can't stop talking about themselves. They want to hire someone who they connect with and who understands the problems their business is facing. If you have something to offer, it will be obvious in how you engage that discussion.

Outreach to Individuals

There are two different approaches to outreach. I know a lot of folks like to launch newsletters, but people already have a lot of mail filling their inboxes, and unless your newsletter has something really pertinent to those on your mailing list, it's just junk (and potentially annoying).

What I have found more effective is to make regular, personal contacts. If you've begun to make some connections with people who are in your bull's-eye category of clients, mark your calendar to stay connected to them and on their mind. For example, if when you last spoke, they indicated to keep in touch, ask them, should

I reach out next quarter? (Quarters are a good interval because it's not too far away but it's also not in 20 workdays, which isn't enough time for action to happen.) For people on your core client list, quarterly or biannual connection is pretty key. Keep track of your connections with individuals. This communication is important: It is the center of relationships, including remembering important details about the people who are central to your work. When you meet with people over breakfast, lunch, dinner/coffee, the point isn't so much to sell yourself as to stay abreast of their work, to take a genuine interest in what they're doing.

Also, it's good to be open about the work you're doing—what you like about it and what's a challenge. Authenticity is at the core of any good relationship, including your business relationships. I'm not by any means suggesting you complain about any work or clients (though I admit I've done this and always regretted it), but you can ask in confidence for input on challenges or insight into your work. Even though the meeting is not about sales, it's good for people that you meet up with to understand what you *want* to do more of and what you are *good* at doing. So, have that three-sentence elevator pitch in your back pocket at all times.

Once a relationship has been established and enough trust has been built, it is time to explicitly say that you're seeking leads: "I'm trying to expand my business next quarter, year, half year— do you have any suggestions?" Or even more intentionally, "I'm quite interested in doing more work with companies like X—do you have any relationships in that space?" Pause, discuss. "Would you be comfortable referring me to X?"

It is critical to carefully track your contacts and what you have learned from them. You can buy tools for this purpose, but a simple spreadsheet has been my biggest and best tool over the many years that I've been in business by myself full-time. This spreadsheet tracks all of my business relationships and all of my contacts. To download a free resource, go to my website, http://www.createtheworkyouwant.com/, and select the file for start-up contact tracking.

After each meeting, you can open up this contact-tracking list and add columns for the date of contact and notes. The best part about having the contact list in a simple spreadsheet is that when your business explodes and you have 100 contacts, you can then buy your first CRM (customer relationship management) software and simply transport the data from your spreadsheet to the new mode of managing your contacts and customer relationships.

Lastly, following up with clients that have full-time jobs listed can be valuable. The creation of a new position is often an indication of immediate internal needs. Your question is: Can you address that need in a focused short-term approach? For example, could you train and develop others' capacity within existing staff? Is there something driving the need for a full-time person that could be addressed by having an outside consultant manage and execute project work (e.g. completing short-term research or strategy work, running a competitive process, running a hiring process for an organization, working on fundraising, or building a communications campaign)? If you're made aware of a job in a company whose pressing needs you could meet, start by inquiring if you could support the need with a three-day-a-week contract instead for X weeks or months.

Summary

So how do you find and keep your clients? Develop a list of potential clients, attend functions where you can rub shoulders with them, foster those relationships, and carefully track contact information. Clients are essential—no business exists without them.

Connecting with Your People

My mission in life is not merely to survive, but to thrive; and to do so with some passion, some compassion, some humor, and some style.
—Maya Angelou

Yes, you need clients, but you also need others in order for you and your business to thrive. Connecting with your people is a critical step in being successful as a solo consultant. This is not because you don't have the capability of creating your business with the resources you already own; rather, people and networks are a source of energy, creativity, and resources—they can channel more opportunities and connections. Each of us needs a "high-value" network. This web of connections will look different for each person depending on your business and your personality. If you're going to work long-term on your own, then you must figure out how to thrive flying solo, and a high-value network is the key to unlocking this potential.

What does it mean to thrive? The Merriam-Webster dictionary says that to thrive is "to grow vigorously, and to flourish." While personal thriving may not be your driving concern as you launch your business, I promise you, it will become a concern rather quickly if you don't give it some thought.

Building a High-Value Network for Support

For me, a high-value network is composed of those I want to learn from and whose input I want on my life and my business. These are also people whom I care about deeply and whose success matters to me. It's a give and take. Having this high-value network is one of the ways that you will successfully stay in business for the long haul. Here's why: Sometimes you just need people. I have colleagues who would step in for me in a pinch, when things go wrong with the business, a contract is falling apart, or I'm having a conflict with a subcontractor, I turn to my network for trusted, confidential advice (or just to vent).

Another reason that I maintain this network is because I really like these people—they are friends and mentors and colleagues. Sometimes I even seek out ways for us to do business together. By staying intentionally connected, I have a better sense of what they're passionate about, what expertise they have, and where opportunities may intersect for us. We all need a tribe of some kind, but when you're self-employed, you have to build it for yourself with great intention. In some ways, working for a company provides an easier path as your colleagues are built in—but you can't pick and choose your close colleagues. When you're self-employed, however, you get to construct your perfect team and network of advisors. In my experience, these are the groups that should be in your network.

Work colleagues/partners

Some of my best and closest colleagues have been the individuals who have worked with me on the various projects that I've obtained or that we've bid on together. Whereas we have no formal ongoing connection, we've worked together enough on either quick/short-term projects or big/multiyear projects that we have a good sense of each other's working style. Fairly regularly I will call one of these people for input on a problem or to figure out something related to work. But I also make a point of intentionally engaging with these individuals—knowing about their lives, sharing a meal together when possible, acknowledging important milestones (birthdays, holidays, work achievements), and exploring ideas together. Make time for colleagues and partners in your work, even when you're not sharing a current project together.

Competitors/partners

Perhaps the most impactful thing I did to make my business less solitary was to partner with others. This collaboration has looked different at various stages, but early on I would talk with clients about projects, then go back to the budget and build in time for a key partner. Sometimes that partner helped provide data collection or part of the analysis work, but at other times I simply brought in a full partner with shared expertise. Much to my surprise, clients were happy to have two experts, or a team, working on their problems with them. In some scenarios I would even bring these partners in at the very start of the work so that we could strategize together. Just remember that when you are partnering with someone, be clear about how each party will benefit and in what ways, especially when you are co-bidding a project.

At other times, I've found myself in the middle of a project that I was contracted to do solo, but I became stuck, for whatever reason—sometimes boredom, sometimes my own procrastination. In these cases, I hired subcontractors to help me. I've hired people to write summaries, find literature and research a topic, write a presentation, create visuals for a presentation, transcribe interviews I've conducted and summarize key findings, or to write an initial draft of something. I don't always use the content that these short-term subcontractors have created, but I've found that the process of hiring someone and explaining the work to them— and then discussing and critiquing the work they've provided—is enough to ignite my brain on the topic. This hiring does not need to be an expensive endeavor—you can find people on sites like Fiverr and UpWork for very little money. I've also hired graduate students who are seeking some professional experience to do this kind of work for me.

Whereas I like to be open—and many in the contract field are quite open about their rates and bids—competition can create some awkward situations. For example, you might learn about a contracting opportunity because someone you know is competing for it, or you might hear about an opportunity from a colleague.

The good news: There is plenty of work to go around the world. Your competitors need to be your colleagues; otherwise, it's going to be a very lonely world for you. This reality means that you should get to know others who are doing what you're doing.

See them as colleagues and people with whom to collaborate. One day you will have a project bigger than yourself (or they will), and you'll be calling each other for help.

Of course, use some discretion—perhaps you shouldn't share every aspect of your business with a close competitor colleague in your field. I once made the mistake of sharing open competition opportunities I was considering with colleagues. They ended up competing against me, and I lost to them. I recommend discussing only work that you currently have in contract (assuming it's not private information). But among many of my self-employed colleagues, we do share information such as what we charge clients and what we include in contracts. We reach out to one another for advice on problem contracts. We also support and root for each other in what we're trying to achieve and offer business advice.

Informal mentoring relationships

All of us need some mentoring, but few people actually seek this out with intention. One way to achieve a constructive mentoring relationship is to simply be open to it. As you walk through your day-to-day life, you will come across people who are doing amazing things. It is natural to feel intimidated and inspired by these achievements, particularly by people who are senior to you in your professional world. But it's important to pay attention to these encounters because they can lead to the most amazing mentoring connections.

Over the years, I have been fortunate to have exceptional mentors. I'm grateful for these relationships. One simple way to form these relationships is to reach out to someone you've met during a meeting. Re-introduce yourself—indicate who you are and what you do and that you'd be interested in learning more about their work and their professional path and to get input on the same in your life. This is key: You have to indicate that the intention is not only learning about them but also gaining their input on your professional goals. People genuinely feel honored by such an invitation, and if it's not something they have time for, they will let you know. I know from experience that each time a person who is earlier on their professional path asks me to talk by phone or over coffee, I'm always happy to do it. I see these en-counters as an opportunity to give back after years of receiving this kind of investment from others, and I feel honored and hum-bled that someone wants my input. Today, it's quite easy to make these connections because a simple in-person meeting can be fol-lowed up via email or LinkedIn or social media.

If someone that you see as a mentor gives you the opportunity to meet with them in person and to learn from them, you abso-lutely must soak it up. Glean all that you can in terms of learning out of that meeting. You will be sitting across from a person with exceptional wisdom, and they are carving time out of their busy schedule for you. Go into these appointments with objectives: Be prepared with what you want to discuss and what questions to ask.

Most importantly, you cannot go into these appointments pretending to have it all together. You don't want the mentor to walk away thinking, "Wow, he/she seems to have it all figured out already." That would be a wasted opportunity. Be intentional about getting input on your professional work. I've had mentors help me think through difficult questions such as the following: "Lately, the biggest challenge with my work has been X—what do you think?" Or, "I really want to expand my work to include more of X, but what are your thoughts?" Or, "I see the future opportunities for me being somewhere in the arena of X—is that a burgeoning area?".

Try to keep the conversation positive (though admittedly I have had my moments of ranting). The key strategy is to limit your own talking so that you can get the mentor's input. You have to ask, and then you have to listen.

Professional coaches

There will be phases of your professional life when access to rich relationships with colleagues and mentors are less frequent for whatever reason, or where the issues you're navigating are too complex to discuss over a lunch appointment or phone call. For me, this phase occurred when my children were quite small: I was working from home more frequently and struggling with the direction of my business. During these questioning periods, a professional coach can be a lifesaver. The best way to find a quality coach is by asking the people you know for recommendations. I have used professional coaches to help me sort out business direction, to organize and work through issues with my bookkeeping and financial forecasting, and to help me be more productive.

Professional back office team

From the very beginning of launching my business, I needed a number of professional supports. Depending on what kinds of projects I've had, my needs have ebbed and flowed; but I wanted to be smart about my time from the onset. When I had a project where I had to conduct 20 site visits, coordinating travel for all of them was not a smart use of my time. Instead I hired an hourly

administrative support person who understood my travel preferences and could build itineraries and schedule my visits. With
another one of my early clients, the budgeting became pretty
complex with expenses and subcontractors, so I took the recommendations of a coach and began working with an hourly
bookkeeper. Ten years later, this person is still supporting my
work, even helping me on personal financial planning and administrative tasks. I have been fortunate to find people who were good
team members and a good professional fit.

Even though you work as a solo shop, you still need a professional team. This team will make your *life* work. Your time as a
contractor is so valuable. You are the one who makes the business
happen, and you are the one often executing the work and managing teams, so you can't also be the one doing every other part of
the business. Early in my consulting career, I produced a high
volume of report publications. I needed to have good editors,
proofreaders, fact-checkers, layout/designer folks, and in some
cases graphic artists, who could help me produce final products
quickly. Fiverr and Upwork are both great resources for hiring
short-term support for some of these items, but ultimately you
will want to have a bench of people whose skills and availability
you can predict.

Think about this team from the start—learn about contractors doing work you might need. Will you need people in editing/
copyediting, design, analytics, ghostwriting, creative, marketing,
communications, virtual assistant services, project management,
finances? What about travel supports or administrative tasks?

Taking this assistance a step further, what do you need to
make your work life coincide with your personal life in ways that
help you to be more productive? What is the thing that distracts

you from work? When I was working from home with little kids, it was the organization of the house that got in the way—dishes in the sink, laundry, dinner prep. My solution was a childcare provider who would come to the house and manage all of those things. Perhaps all you need is someone to do the laundry or cook food a few days a week. Think about what is sucking up your time and energy and distracting you from being productive during the day. Sure, paying for this help was a financial stretch for me at times, but it meant that precious working hours were not spent on these things; I was able to work from home undistracted by the long household to-do list. Ultimately, having me work more efficiently was the best financial decision for my family and me.

Not Fitting In

Even though you may have this network of people who are part of your working life, as a self-employed consultant you may feel as if you don't really fit in anywhere. It's a feeling that you have to acclimate to as an independent operator. Even though working for yourself is increasingly common, this work mode is still on the margins as a chosen path. It's important to just embrace it. Eventually you will find your niche and how you fit (and more importantly how it fits you). Human beings want to belong to a tribe of some kind, and I can assure you that the longer you pursue this independent business endeavor, you will find your tribe. It might not be at the water cooler or at a company holiday party because you won't necessarily belong to any one entity. Instead, you might attend multiple holiday parties and engage in the water cooler conversations at many companies. You may also find that it's awfully nice to not be tethered to any one business.

If fitting in is something that is important to you, you'll need to give some thought as to where you can find community. In my work, these places of belonging have varied over the years. Early on, it was important for me to be a member of the professional association of others doing research in my field, but over time I found that I wanted more affiliation with people who were business growers and developers, so I found more camaraderie among entrepreneurs. Today I'm finding a great sense of community among other women business owners and professional services consultants.

Because I don't have the regularity of seeing people at the office, I have to be intentional about the relationships that I want to invest in and how I want to develop them. Who is at the core of your personal and professional community? How will you stay connected to these people, and how often? On your annual calendar, note times for making plans with them. Relationships, both personal and professional, do not happen on accident. These connections require intention, some vulnerability, and some give-and-take: You're not just friends with people to have them care for your needs but to genuinely care for them as well.

Working Alone

I'm a fairly extroverted person. If I interacted with 100 people over the course of a day, that would not be too many. Interacting with new people invigorates me. Consequently, the isolation that I felt early on in my business quickly became a problem for me. Some periods have been more challenging than others, but I've learned a few hacks that have helped.

First, working 100% alone and continuing to be productive was going to be impossible for me. So from the very beginning, my work had to have a social component. Here are some solutions:

- *Work on site.* One of my early nonprofit clients hired me for a 15-hour per week consulting engagement. I knew they had plentiful office space and so I asked if they'd provide me a space. With that dedicated space, I was able to "move in" and use that space multiple times per week. The proximity yielded amazing opportunities to engage with the organization's leader and get to know key players, ultimately landing additional consulting opportunities for me.

- *Schedule in-person meetings.* The temptation to do everything by phone or videoconference is ever present. For some of you, this the business model will be essential, as your clients may be reluctant to ask their consultants to travel and won't suggest in-person meetings. But it's often welcome if I say, "I'm already going to be downtown (or in your city next month, etc.), so why don't we meet in person?"

- *Plan Meals, Coffee & Tea, Drinks.* More often than not, clients and their teams welcome the chance to get to know consultants better outside of work meetings. When the timing is appropriate, try to arrange opportunities for connection outside of work meetings. This is a real opportunity to get to know people minus an agenda (you already have the job).

- *Connect Groups of Contractors.* If you're feeling like you have no groups of support, it might be time to connect with other contractors and consultants who are working in the same capacity as you. At my field's annual meeting, independent evaluators have a dinner where I make a point of connecting with others in my geographic region.

- *Join a Networking Group.* Find out what networking groups others in your field or among your clients join, and sign up. Get on the email lists and in their Meetup groups and plug in. If there is literally no group of people doing what you do, consider starting one. It doesn't take much time or effort: You could gather a group of individuals virtually for a quarterly well-structured call to start engaging intentionally with colleagues in your same area.

- *Pay to Join a Professional Association.* Almost every field has a professional association of some kind. If you have literally none, you can join your local Chamber of Commerce or a local Small Business Association.

- *Join a Co-Working Space.* Today, many different options for working in a shared workspace are available to self-employed, "solopreneurs"—(e.g. WeWork, MakeOffices, Cove, etc.). Many of these companies offer a low-cost membership, even for light use, with access to the entire local community, including message boards and events.

- *Use FaceTime, Google Hangout, Skype, Zoom.* All of the technology available today provides a wealth of opportunities to connect visually. Several of my colleagues know that I love to see their faces when we are communicating. Not only do these mediums facilitate a personal connection, but you also know that others are in this work with you.

Summary

Just do it. Connect with your people—your partners, competitors, mentors, coaches, and back-office team. Find professional communities, either in actual or virtual space. You can be your own boss without being alone.

Creating a Workspace and Approach That Fits

If you're going to stay the path of working for yourself, the most important thing to navigate (after you actually begin to obtain contracts) is how to stay productive. This chapter is all about your workspace and work approach. If you can't crack this nut, you won't be in business for very long. In this chapter, I am going to offer a long list of tips and tricks that I've learned, but ultimately every path is unique. What worked for me may not work for you, but you can use these ideas to spur the development of productivity strategies right for you.

First and Foremost, You Actually Have to be Productive

While most of America goes off to work to an office where they report in to some defined set of hours, space, culture, and other obligations, a huge number of us are just working on our own at home. Entrepreneurship is a growing way of life as startups and pop-ups emerge in every corner of the country. With the low costs of technology and the ease of remote work, a growing share of people are working for companies as freelancers and consultants. For millions of these people, those businesses run right from their own homes.

When I first launched my research business, I assumed that eventually I would hire full-time employees and operate a multi-million-dollar budget. As it turns out, the success of the company has been its flexibility as a single-owned LLC firm that hires sub-contractors as researchers with specialized expertise to suit the needs of respective clients and projects. Whereas the work projects over these years have ranged from a few days to a few years of engagement, and a few thousand dollars to a million, the reality is that my 20-person research firm dream did not become my business model these last ten years.

Being an extreme extrovert who thrives on being around others, I had to tackle the question: How do I move forward with my work and stay focused and motivated, day-to-day, when most of the time I am flying solo? I'm not going to proceed through this chapter and pretend to have it all figured out. I will say that I've learned a lot from what doesn't work. I have spent big gaps of time surfing Redfin real estate opportunities, watching Netflix, and obsessively organizing my kitchen cupboards.

But as the years have passed and I've settled into a practice of working alone, I have learned many tricks. One of the most important things I've learned is that productivity ebbs and flows for all of us. It varies by time of day, season of life, and the types of tasks at hand. No one is productive 100% of the time, and we should all both schedule periods of lower expected productivity (e.g. following business travel) and embrace unscheduled bouts of low productivity without negative self-talk. Welcome the moments of no productivity; don't struggle against it. In fact, as you figure out where and when you are most energetic, begin to actually schedule time to do absolutely nothing on occasion during those high-energy periods. The reality is that the creative parts of our brain need this space to think, feel, get restored, and take pleasure in life and work.

Still, as the days, weeks, months, and years roll by, you will need to find a system for keeping yourself productive and energized. Below are key factors that have fostered my productivity over the years.

Work Calendar

To be consistently productive, be methodical about your work calendar. Think about the cycle of your work life and personal life. How does your professional rhythm ebb and flow, and at what times do you need to be focused and working? When should you be focused on business development? When will you carve out time for managing money? Where are the natural touch points for reflection in your year?

Much of my work is related to higher education, so the winter break and the end of summer are natural points for planning. At the beginning of each year, I try to build these planning blocks into my calendar. I also build in times for doing administrative work and financial work, analysis, and reflection. I've also loved following online Facebook communities with a focus on productivity and attending at least one in-person conference where I connect with other entrepreneurs.

Since working from examples can be invaluable, below is a list of my regular calendar items—scheduled activities that you may want to include on your own calendar.

- Mid-month: Fully clean out email inbox, pay bills, and process personal paperwork and mail.
- Last day of the month: Review time sheets. Send out all invoices.
- Reserve a half day to a full day for the following activities in these months:
    - January: Use one full day to plan a yearlong calendar based on my new year's goals.
    - February: Plan and organize for April tax filing.
    - March: Take a vacation.
    - April: Review progress on goals; adjust as needed.
    - May: Engage in personal financial planning.
    - June: Take a vacation.
    - July: Review progress on goals; adjust as needed.
    - August: Plan for fall, incorporating kids' schedules, childcare, domestic help.
    - September: Take a vacation.
    - October: Review progress on goals; adjust as needed.
    - November: Review personal financial planning goals.
    - December: Attend a learning or professional development event of some kind or take a weekend away for planning and reflection.

There are so many approaches to one's calendars, but the key thing is to map out time for these "wellness" activities and commit to these plans.

As you grow your clientele, you will need a yearlong calendar to sketch out when you will accomplish all the work to which you've committed. If you're planning a vacation or have to attend to a major personal event, you will have fewer work hours in a given week, month or quarter. It's important to have a clear sense of when you're available for client work so you don't miss promised deadlines.

Personal Accountability

One of the biggest challenges to your productivity is not having accountability from anyone, so you have to just build it in. Here are ideas for you to try:

- Tell a colleague or client that you'd like them to review something by a certain time. Deliver that work on time because you are a person of your word and because you asked them to carve out time to review something for you.
- Get together with others to get things done. On occasion I have reached out to colleagues to say, "Hey, I'm really struggling to make progress on a project. Could we get together to discuss it or could we chat on the phone about it?" Or, "Would you mind looking over some of my ideas on how to move forward?" I've even gone over to a friend's house for the day and worked at her dining room table just to keep myself moving forward.

- Find another self-employed person and create a formal accountability relationship. On Mondays, you can touch base to discuss your plans for the week. At midweek, share an update with each other. At the end of the week, discuss what your accomplishments were and what you'd like to do better next week.

- Hire people to work with you on something. This is a favorite tactic of mine because it keeps me moving forward on a project with a specific timeline. I can touch base with this person at the beginning of the week and establish some specific deadlines. I'm essentially creating an obligation to someone else at a cost to me, but it helps get my brain moving on a project that I'm avoiding.

- Carve out blocks in your calendar for specific work that you need to do that is not urgent. This is the best way to ensure that you will not procrastinate on something for weeks and months and then create a situation where you're doing sloppy, last-minute work.

Pay a professional coach if you can't crack your productivity problems. You can use a coach just to hold you accountable, deal with creative blocks, and help you improve your work habits. Meet or chat with the coach once per week or biweekly for a period of time. Set intentions on the things you need to accomplish.

As a partner in a Washington, D.C., international marketing company, Julie arranges her day to cater to her international clients and to maximize her productivity. First thing after rising around 6 a.m., she checks her email to respond to across-the-globe clients whose workday may be coming to a close. In the morning, she engages in business development work with her European clients (during their afternoons). Julie focuses on projects in the afternoon, followed by administration tasks at the end of the day when her juices are slowing down. Her clients' time zones help her chunk her day into activities that all need to get done.

At the end of the day, accountability is about following through on a promise, not just to others but also to yourself. When you are unsuccessful, don't beat yourself up. Learn from the mistake and develop a new plan for tackling the productivity challenge the next day.

Professional Development: Spend Your Money on It

Now that you work for yourself, you still need to figure out where and how to get the professional development that you need. This growth investment is costly, I'm aware. But it's a necessity. Reserve a budget for travel and events that can help you stretch yourself professionally. On occasion, I have attended pre-conference intensives to get further training or acquire new tools in my field. I've found these sessions to be more useful than conferences because there is more opportunity for close connections and the content is often presented in half-day or full-day sessions (vs. wandering through a big conference catalogue trying to figure out which sessions are most useful).

Today you can find many opportunities for doing online courses, taking seminars, and joining other professional gatherings without even leaving your home or office. You can do post-baccalaureate programs online, short-term certification and certificate programs, or open education resources like Coursera. You can sign up for webinars and telecasts of many events without paying to attend them. I like listening to short items like Ted Talks and all kinds of amazing podcasts. Opportunities to learn abound in the online spaces of our age. You really have no reason that you can't invest in your own professional development, even if you have virtually no budget at all.

Some of us realize that our skills and training need updating as we pursue this path to self-employment. For those of us who went to college many years ago, there are a ton of new skills that we still need to acquire. This retraining is perfectly fine and in line with the workforce trends of retooling in any career. Perhaps you never completed any formal education, but you've worked hard and enjoyed a satisfying career trajectory without it. You will need additional training to grow further or into different arenas if your field is evolving, or perhaps you will need to earn a degree later in life.

In today's world, skills updating is a part of life. No one in any career has all the skills they need to be effective in their work forever. Ongoing training and retooling are absolutely essential. In fact, this willingness to keep learning is what sets apart individuals who can ultimately become superb professional services consultants. But retooling is not something that should stop you from getting started in your work today. You can build your business on the skills that you currently have and update your skills and education as you go. The greatest asset that you have is yourself. Your mind, creativity, passion, drive, energy, and skills—these assets are enough to build your business; therefore, protect and grow that asset right along with your business.

Personal Growth

If you don't have a habit for personal growth, get one. It is 100% necessary. There will be no one else, no supervisor, concerned about your growth and future opportunities. It all comes down to you. Your professional future is purely your responsibility.

If that charge sounds daunting to you, it should. Most people follow a defined path in their professional field, seeking out defined training and experiential opportunities. Their supervisors provide them advancement opportunities. But you need to create these opportunities for yourself. You must begin with having a growth mindset: See yourself as someone who wants to be constantly learning and developing. If you don't invest in this kind of ongoing development, you will become stagnant both personally and professionally. What this daily practice looks like may vary, but you need to carve out time for your ongoing learning and reflection.

In terms of my own growth, I have been strongly influenced by Hal Elrod's *The Miracle Morning*. His approach has shaped how I launch my day, and I recommend it to everyone seeking growth opportunities in their lives, both personal and professional. Ask yourself a few key questions:

- What area of life do I want to grow in this year?
- In what areas of work do I need to learn more?
- Where could I use some coaching/training?

Answering these questions has led me to read books on productivity, money, relationships, and in my field of research and evaluation. I build time into my schedule to stay abreast of the latest books and research in my field, reading works by those who are thought leaders in my professional world. I also keep an ongoing hit list on my phone—things I want to read, things I want to listen to (podcasts, Ted talks), and things that I want to watch (movies, in particular). I love to watch inspiring movies with my daughters, including documentaries or sports movies that show the grit and challenges athletes face in achieving amazing physical feats.

Launching your own business is the perfect opportunity to refocus your efforts on both professional and personal growth. This effort will help you be successful. Yes, the process of creating something new, like a business, is by nature trial-and-error learning—but you can learn from many external resources as well. Try to remove the language from your mind about what you're good at or bad at—everyone has strengths and weaknesses. Instead, think through what you need to learn. Of course, functioning from our strengths is useful, but when you're launching a business, you often have to perform all the functions on your own at the start.

Recalibrate your thinking to a setting where you can learn anything. Instead of avoiding the challenging aspects, embrace them. Know you can get help by enlisting others to teach you or coach you, reading about an issue, watching how-to videos, practicing a skill that you have to grow in, and simply trying. If you're entering into this phase of your business life, saying things like "I'm just not good at X" or "I'm not confident about my skills in X" or "I'm just not a person who does X (sales, money, etc.)," then it's time for a reset.

Move Your Body to Keep Your Mind Healthy

If you're working for yourself for the first time and creating your own schedule, then building in time for exercise is going to be critical to your longevity. Because you don't have a boss expecting you to clock in at a certain time or work until a particular hour, you have a great deal of freedom to structure your life in any way you want.

Hitting the weights in the middle of the day when my gym is empty has been my ticket to fitness. At times I've worked out with a trainer or taken a class of some kind, but ultimately, I love the peacefulness of the empty gym. Others are at the gym first thing in their day, but mornings are a time when I like to read, have my coffee, and then go for a walk outside. Perhaps for you this is a morning bike ride, or a run, or a workout on your at-home cardio machine, but just get your heart pumping for 30 minutes in the early part of your day. On the days when I'm headed for the gym, I generally work in my gym clothes so I'm ready to dash out the door; I shower up as soon as get home. I want to avoid being home working in pajamas or sweatpants all day, and building in the daily workout is the best way to make that happen.

Kate works from home offering editing services, as well as communications strategy and training. To ensure her social and physical wellness, she became a barre instructor, leading regular fitness classes in her community. These classes keep her balanced and sane, with the perk of bringing in a little extra income.

Even if you can't join a club, break up your day with stretches, a yoga video, or a walk in your neighborhood. Your body, mind, and spirit will thank you.

Figure Out Your Workspace

Where you choose to create a workspace is personal and closely related to what will make you most productive. You know yourself: Where are you most productive? What environment energizes you and feeds your creativity? What does it take for you to focus?

The answers vary for all of us. During some time periods, renting an office space was completely necessary for me. When my kids were small, I needed different things during different years. When they were babies, I wanted to see them throughout the day and take breaks to feed them. But when they were mobile and loud and I could hear them from any room in the house and they knew when I was there, I had to work outside of the home. Later, when they became school age, it was much more convenient to work from a home office. I also had a travel schedule involving many nights on the road, and the cost of an office just didn't make sense.

What has worked for Mike, our urban designer mentioned in Chapter 3, is to both live and work in what he calls a "live/work unit." Typical to the old-fashioned main street, he operates his business on the street level and resides in the floor above. The ground floor also has room for four employees to work alongside him. For Mike, the greatest advantages to this arrangement are paying just one mortgage and not having to commute to work.

Working from home may or may not work for you. When you are working from home, all your productivity tricks need to be in motion because you want to be sure that your home office is energizing. If you don't have a home large enough for a dedicated workroom, create a space dedicated to work and fill it with things that will help you focus.

Come Up With a Plan for Digital Distractions

We live in an age of distraction. Everything around us, whether you're working from home or from a shared office space, calls (or beeps) for our attention. You need a plan to address these hazards. What are the biggest distractions in your daily life? Take them by the reigns by developing rules for these things. Here are some productively hacks that I use with regard to digital attention-grabbers.

Make creative time internet free

Most of us are connected 100% of the time to an electronic device. Even in meetings I am often using devices to record things, to take notes, or to schedule. It's not usually realistic to turn these things off all day, but when you have creative work to do, they need to get put away. This rule applies any time I need to write anything, think through a complicated problem, review comments on something I've written and need to edit/rewrite, or design a presentation flow (not constructing the slides but thinking about talking points).

To shut down this distraction, I simple reach up to those little Wi-Fi bars on my computer and turn off the connection. Next, I turn off my phone or put it in airplane mode and place it on another floor of my house or away in my bag (if I'm out of the office). Wonderful things happen during these periods of being offline. If you're not unplugging a bit each day, it's likely that you're far too distracted. I try to work in 50-minute blocks, but typically once I get started on one of these offline creative times, I become so absorbed with what I'm doing that much more than an hour of time can pass before I glance at my phone. Typically, the phone is an easy quick check: Have the kids needed me? Have I missed potentially important calls or texts? But if nothing urgent appears, I'll often stretch my legs or change position to standing or sitting depending on where I began, get some water, and move on to another block of concentrated time. The trick is to *not* check email, a rule that brings me to my next point.

Manage email distractions

Determine the number of times you will check email each day and how you will manage it. I run my business from email, so if messages are left in my inbox, it's often because I've left them there as a reminder to do something later. More than 25 messages in my email inbox is an indication that my work life is out of control. I use a few simple rules to keep email working for me:

- All business messages are executed using my business email account (correspondence with clients, subcontractors, etc.).
- Business mail gets checked twice a day: once midmorning and once after midafternoon. The absolute worst thing you can do to start your day is open your mail and check your messages. Period. If you start your day this way, you have jeopardized your day's productivity. You should have identified the day before what is going to be the priority for the next morning. It should be the first and only thing you tackle when you hit your desk (if you work at a desk).

Once you've accomplished this task, you can move on to your messages.

- Highlight/flag things that are urgent and have to be responded to that day. Make a note wherever you make to-do lists about these necessary responses. I use an electronic checklist for my day divided by AM/PM. If it's something that requires a response but isn't urgent, add it to your calendar for another day. Simply respond to the person about when you'll get back to them and file the email away in a folder for that client.

- Personal bills, subscriptions of any kind, stores, travel, and any other messages are tied to my personal email account. This separation keeps me from being constantly distracted by personal stuff or tempted to begin shopping in the middle of the afternoon. It's not that those personal messages are unimportant; on the contrary, critical stuff is in there from my kids' school announcements to upcoming travel details to some pretty good sales. Reserve non-work times for reviewing these personal items toward the end of the day.

Control mobile devices

Your beloved phone—Android, Google phone, or whatever it is that you love—may be hurting your productivity rather than helping it. I love my mobile device in the dead of August, when I'm at the beach with my kids, and once a day I have a way to check in and make sure all systems are running smoothly. But on a day-to-day basis in the office, my phone is an enormous distraction. Today most people schedule business calls, so unless you're under the gun with an imminent event or deadline where you need to be reached 24/7, it's a good idea to just turn your phone off fully for some periods of time. I recommend "off" because powering down and stowing away a phone is just enough of a nuisance to resume use that you might actually ignore it. Simply flipping off the sound or turning it over may not do the trick. Consider having some phone-free periods of time in your day or week.

Turn stuff off

Always turn off mobile device sounds and put them out of reach when you are with clients and employees/contractors. Nothing is worse than meeting with someone who watches their phone or looks every time it dings or vibrates. It's awful. There is no better way to make the person you're with feel disconnected from you and disrespected by you. I know that many of you are caregivers who need to be reached, and that's fine. Today most smart phones have features where you can put your phone on silent for set hours but whitelist certain contacts for incoming texts and calls. Realistically, the odds are quite slim that a real emergency is going to occur. Truly being present and connecting to those you're with in the moment makes you a far more effective (and kind) human being.

Wrangle in Facebook, Instagram, and other online tools

Social media and other online tools are a blessing and curse. They help us to grow our businesses by creating personal and professional networks, and they can be an amazing way to stay connected to those we care about in our lives. But they can also suck the life out of our productivity. Try loading a time-tracking app onto your phone for your working hours to see how much time you spend on social media in a given month. My downfall is real estate sites—I just love tracking what's happening in my favorite neighborhoods. I can get lost for an hour just perusing prices and profiles and checking out pictures. What I've come to admit is that this process is my form of avoidance—skirting something I don't like about my day, my week, or sometimes my life. It's a bit of an escape for me as well as a pleasure. But when I catch myself going there, I have to take a moment away from everything to reflect on what the escape is all about and address it.

For many of us, these online distractions are simply a bit of pleasure on days when work seems less interesting. Attending to these sites is fine, but I would recommend that you switch to some-time in the evening (or when you're not trying to be productive). My best days are the ones that begin with leaving my phone plugged in and at my bedside. I head downstairs and do my morning routine (coffee, brief meditation, review of my goals and priorities, pages in my current book that I'm reviewing for personal learning, and some writing or journaling about what I'm thinking about or am grateful for that day). Then I'm out for my walk. Typically, nothing critical is happening in my personal or professional life between 10 p.m. and 8 a.m.; and nothing is happening on social media that I *need* to know before launching my day.

Turn off pop-up news and other unnecessary notifications

The news cycle can enter into your mental space at all moments in the day. But if you're like me, these announcements are an enormous emotional drain. They capture your attention, and suddenly you're contemplating the consequences of some news headline that needs investigating. The next thing you know, your day is way off course because of the most recent madness. Yes, we all want to stay informed about national and global issues, but unless your business is in the news media, I'd recommend turning off whatever you read and watch during your most productive hours of the day.

Here is how news access works in our house: Once the kids are up and dressed, we listen to the *Up First* podcast on NPR to catch a quick round-up of the daily news. Later that day when I'm taking a break, I'll read items of interest on my *New York Times* or *Washington Post* online accounts. Occasionally, I'll watch an evening news show. I am a regular consumer of magazines (in the evening) and newspapers (on the weekends), but I try to reserve these media feeds for non-work hours.

Summary

So how do you create a workspace and work rhythm that maximizes your productivity?

- Plan opportunities for personal growth.
- Plot your monthly and yearly calendar.
- Build in personal accountability.
- Find opportunities for professional development.
- Incorporate physical fitness.
- Find a suitable workspace.
- Limit digital distractions.

These efforts will be rewarded in terms of both professional success and personal satisfaction.

Digging Into the Details on Pricing and Budgeting

A top question for those who are launching their professional services business is about how to price. Perhaps they have been offered a contract or know a company that wants to hire them, but they are uneasy about asking too high or too low. Your virgin bid may not be the best time to shoot for the moon, especially if no one can attest to your value in the particular space that you're working. But if you're a seasoned professional, then the high ask might be exactly what you should propose out of the gate. Most people undervalue their time and don't ask for enough money. You need to know your value in your market and rely on your relationships and references. If people know you to be a high-value individual in your market and you're about to launch that value for a fee for the very first time, then reflecting that value in your pricing right from the start is important.

Pricing Your Work

Find out from those you know in related industries what they pay their contractors. This contact could be a colleague or friend who is not a potential client but does hire contractors to do something similar to you. When I was first starting out, I did not ask what others were being paid but thought about what I wanted to be paid. This was a big mistake. Almost a year later, I realized that larger research firms with big overheads were garnering a far higher hourly rate for their most inexperienced research staff, and senior people were getting three times the rate I had asked.

I accessed this information by working on a project for a client who needed external support managing their RFP (request for proposal) process for a big research study. I ended up providing an invaluable service to the company by managing a process that was pretty new to them. Managing that RFP gave me insight into how others presented their work and their budgets. For the first time, I realized that I had the ability to compete with any size firm. They had nothing special in their secret sauce. They had senior-level people supervising with a light touch and lower-level people doing the work. I ended up negotiating that contract with the behemoth research firm, and the client paid me to continue as a research project manager for many more months. This was an incredible learning opportunity for me.

If all else fails, and you can't seem to find out what typical rates are for comparable work, then ask the client. Just know that you may be lowballed. This undervaluing may happen more often for women, young people (or young-looking people), and minorities. This discrimination is disturbing, but I've seen it happen many times as I've witnessed other contractors providing comparable services garnering higher hourly rates.

After leaving full-time employment, Rajesh became a business consultant focusing on human resources. He says that it is easy to be myopic about your own experience: "You have this crisis of confidence about yourself. The temptation is to undervalue your own expertise." But you have to realize that people want to hire you because you have something valuable to offer and that something has a market price. He advises, "That market price is what you should be asking for—nothing more, nothing less."

As you think about hourly rates and daily rates, remember that they are not the same as a salary. You can't take a desired salary and divide it by 52 weeks in the year and make that your daily rate. As a contractor running your own business, you need to remember all of your expenses and unpaid time for business development. Those costs must be built into your daily/hourly fees. As a self-employed person, I still have to pay out of pocket for insurance, subscriptions (industry related and other tools such as Dropbox, Survey Monkey, QuickBooks), business cards, website, email, travel, and most importantly, taxes. I also have to cover time developing my business and any time that I want to take off from work.

Your client, on the other hand, has no cost obligation beyond your fee. They have no obligation to do a big search and selection process for your position, they do not need to contribute to insurance and retirement programs, and they don't have to cover unemployment insurance, training, and onboarding costs for you. What they are paying for with that higher price is your expertise and immediate availability (or negotiated availability) for a fixed project or set of services. You may be surprised to learn that large consulting companies that provide an enormous number of people for short- and long-term services can charge upwards of $300 per hour for their consultants; some individuals with high-level expertise in the financial sector provide analytic support and consultation for well over $1,000 an hour.

Sometimes you will find clients who just have a fixed budget and can't go higher than a certain hourly amount. Hourly and daily rates are not the only reason you should choose to take on a client. As a rookie, you need to factor in several things. Perhaps the client with whom you're negotiating is incredibly important to your future business; he or she will provide a credible reference. Then by all means, negotiate something that works. I'm not saying that you should take on a client at a demoralizing rate, but I'm suggesting that you establish a base rate and take alternative paths to the work. Here are ways to think creatively about compensation:

- Let's say that your rate is $100/ hour, or $800/day, and you've estimated that the assignment is roughly 2-3 days per week for two months. Ask for an agreement that guarantees a minimum amount of days for the work, and make it clear that your rate is $100/hour. But note that you are willing to do two days for $1,600 weekly at your desired rate and one day pro bono for the two-month period. This offer is a way to make your agreement work but not end up with a documented rate far lower than where you know you need to be. Ideally, the client walks away feeling as though they've gotten a deal, and you've been realistic with that company's budget constraints. Additionally, you have an opportunity to knock it out of the park and come away with a strong recommendation.

- Another approach you can take is to accept the lower rate on a project and hire subcontractors to help you get the work done. You are still the person to engage directly with your client, but you find back-office support (less expensive people) to provide services for you. For example, you can pay a good editor to clean up written documents, a graphic designer to lay out papers and presentations, a smart analyst to help you look for and decipher data, a good researcher to help you pull together background documentation, or an administrative assistant to help you book travel, transcribe interviews, or even conduct interviews under your supervision. Some contracts do have a clear stipulation that the named consultant is solely executing the scope of work. Make sure that your contract reflects what you're planning to do.

- Lastly you can agree to a fixed amount of time. Indicate that your regular daily rate is X but that you are open to jumping in on the work for a shorter period at a lower rate (for whatever reasons you have). I do hesitate to even suggest this option because you deserve to be paid for your time. This approach documents you at lower amounts, and at the end of the short period, your client may not be willing to increase the amount. You may open yourself to this approach in exceptional scenarios, such as when you're working on a project for an upcoming grant or investment where you will be a part of the work, or it's the end of the year and the budget has to await renegotiation in the next budget fiscal cycle.

Creating a Project Budget

The process of creating a budget can be daunting, but if you build it in a way that helps you plan the scope of work, it will be a snap. My favorite budget approach, a highly structured one, suits my Type-A personality. The moment I begin thinking about a new project, usually through a conversation with a new client, my mind starts thinking of budgets. Ultimately, the open spreadsheet helps me formulate the work, not the narrative description. It's a simple table structure like the one below (see example 1). You can also download some budgeting resources on my website, http://www.createtheworkyouwant.com/.

Example 1

Dates	Activity	Team Member (1)	Price

I start with the second column: Activity. In this column you're going to begin with the big chunks of work that need to be completed. The example below features a budget that I structured for a company that wanted us to write a report on best practices for building diversity in the pipeline to law schools. It was a relatively small-budget project, so I knew that it wasn't going to include a lot of original data collection. Based on my availability at that time, I also knew that I needed to build in time for a subcontractor. Here are the steps to creating my plan:

1. Under "Activity," list the high-level actions that have to occur to fulfill the contract in column two of your spreadsheet (see example 2).

Example 2

Dates	Activity	Team Member (1) (days required)	Daily Cost (day x daily rate)
	Obtain and review relevant literature		
	Review existing information sources		
	Deliver designed report to client in PDF		
	Present final findings via webinar		

2. Under "Dates," assign dates to each high-level activity. Generally, I use month/year notations unless the client has specified dates for these activities (see example 3).
3. Subdivide each of the high-level activity items into much greater detail (see example 3).

Example 3

Dates	Activity	Team Member (1) (days required)	Daily Cost (day x daily rate)
Dec-19	Obtain and review relevant literature		
	Review and analyze literature		
	Discuss initial analysis and paper plan with client		
Feb-20	Review existing information sources		
	Develop a data base with key information		
	Send a simple survey to select contacts		
	Conduct interviews with 15-20 contacts		
Mar-20	Deliver designed report to client in PDF		
	Write draft 1		
	Obtain input from client and edit		
	Copy edit		
	Design, layout, and proofreading		
Apr-20	Present final findings via webinar		
	Develop presentation materials		

4. Here's where the details really come together: You have to actually estimate how much time it will take to do each of the activities listed (see example 4). I recommend projecting days (not hours). This day estimate goes in the Team Member column; each Team Member gets their own column. In my budgets, this column is usually labeled (Project Manager, Principal Researcher, Co-Principal Researcher, Research Assistant, Data Analyst, etc.). The final column is where you put the calculation of costs by multiplying the day estimates (number in the Team Member column) by the daily rate.

Example 4

Dates	Activity	Team Member (1) (days required)	Daily Cost (day x daily rate)
Dec-19	**Obtain and review relevant literature**		
	Gather all literature and documents	2.00	$1,000
	Review and analyze literature	5.00	$2,500
	Discuss initial analysis and paper plan with client	5.00	$2,500
Feb-20	**Review existing information sources**		
	Develop a data base with key information	0.50	$250
	Send a simple survey to select contacts	2.00	$1,000

	Conduct interviews with 15-20 contacts	4.00	$2,000
Mar-20	**Deliver designed report to client in PDF**		
	Write draft 1	2.00	$1,000
	Obtain input from client and edit	0.50	$250
	Copy edit	0.50	$250
	Design, layout, and proofreading	2.00	$1,000
Apr-20	**Present final findings via webinar**		
	Develop presentation materials	1.00	$500
	SUBTOTAL PERSONNEL EXPENSES	24.50	$12,250

That is a project budget in its simplest form. You can add more columns if you have more team members on a given project. This example assumes that you are the sole person executing the contract. In most cases, in my business, I have several contributors to each budget line. This means that with every task, I have to add in some time for myself to manage the project. For example, if I hire an editor and list the editor's time in the project budget, then I also have to allow some time for managing that piece of the work (the time you spend reaching out to the editor, discussing the project with the editor, and sending documents/reviewing documents). Be sure to allot time for all of these interactions. Further down in the budget, you can have a line item for the actual expenses of editors, designers, communications experts, or whatever else you need.

Once you've completed these personnel estimates, you can create a list of related expenses and add it to the budget total. In my projects, these typically include things like transcription, travel estimates, editorial services, and graphic design services. More recently, I've begun putting in a small percentage of overhead on top of the line for total personnel expenses. I would not recommend including this line when you're first starting out if you're solely providing your own services to the client. However, once your projects begin to grow larger and you have many more expenses for subscriptions and services that require a team, I would recommend adding it as a percentage of your personnel charges to help cover your annual expenses.

Reviewing Legal Agreements

Legal contracts are not the most thrilling documents to review, particularly at the exciting stage of signing on a new client. But a good legal contract can go a long way toward protecting your interests and those of your clients. So, get your handy highlighter and a pen, print out a copy, and dig in over your favorite beverage. You will thank me for telling you to never skip this step.

Read carefully through every contract from start to finish. If you don't understand something, consult an attorney friend or search on the web for clarification. If those options aren't feasible, seek out pro bono clinics for contract review. At times, retaining an attorney is worth the expense. Throughout my career working as a contractor, I've used the services of an attorney on just a few occasions. One was to help me negotiate an enormous multi-year contract. Her advice was well worth the added expense. I used that same attorney to help me establish some template contracts for subcontractors who worked for me as 1099 contractors on that multi-year project and many others. I've also retained an attorney to review complex contracts when I launched work with some very large companies. Sometimes that expertise is just a necessity.

When you're negotiating a contract, keep in mind that it's okay to ask questions. Just because an attorney once upon a time put some wording in a consultant contracting agreement doesn't mean that everything in it applies to you. More often than not, when I've requested something to be stricken from a contract, the reasons are quite obvious and immediately approved. For example, I've had contracts indicate that I would have no intellectual rights to the work product when, in fact, the final reports were to list me as the primary author. Clearly, that exclusion was not the intent of the client. Many times, companies have extraordinary insurance requirements listed in their contracts, too burdensome for a solo contractor but perfectly appropriate for a company of 300 people. These requirements are not necessary in a contract with a professional consultant.

Here are some of the key things that you should look out for and be sure to understand:

- Non-compete clauses that restrict future business
- Insurance requirements
- Work product rights and uses (points about intellectual property in general)
- Liability with regard to company information
- Contract termination detail
- Specified states for the resolution of legal disputes
- Pricing differentials on overtime, if applicable

Summary

Pricing, budgets, and contracts are tricky tasks for a new professional consultant. But they might not be as difficult as you think:

- With pricing, charge what you are worth, but make accommodations when needed to secure advantageous clients.
- When budgeting, move from tasks to dates to time to costs.
- When handed a contract, take the time to review it carefully, noting conditions that are inapplicable or unacceptable.

Enjoy the control that you have in your role as your own boss.

Exploring Approaches to Payment Terms

Many new consultants wonder how to structure payment terms in their new work contracts. Over the years I've taken many approaches, and I've learned a lot along the way. Some contracts are set up to bill hourly, some daily, while others are structured as retainers or fixed budgets with specified payments tied to deliverables or dates. Each approach has its drawbacks and perks. How should you determine the structure of your contract?

To be honest, most of the time it's up to the client. However, I've learned that educating your clients on your preferred contract structure is possible. More often than not, clients can be flexible and just want someone to recommend an approach. Prior to discussing payment terms, you should have fully vetted the project in a contract meeting.

Contract Meetings

Contract negotiation meetings are an important part of ensuring that your work is clearly articulated for the client and for you. Moreover, it's the centerpiece of your getting paid! My preference is to have these conversations in person, with a phone call being a close second. During an in-person meeting, you can get to know someone a bit, get more of a sense of what you think of the other person, and can devote time to listening to their needs. Communicating the nuance of expectations and budget via email is never ideal.

It helps to have in front of you a list of things to discuss. Contract meetings should focus on a few main objectives:

- Learn about the client's preferences regarding how he or she wants to engage with you and stay updated by you throughout the life of the contract. Some of my clients like monthly or bimonthly meetings, some weekly or biweekly. Others just want a periodic email update. Take a minute to consider who the key stakeholders are in a given contract and how each one needs to be kept abreast of the progress. If you're uncertain, you can ask for input at the start of a contract.

- Ask questions to get clarity on the scope of the work. If clarity is lacking, humbly offer some guidance from your expertise about how to execute the work. Clients sometimes need your help figuring out where to go next. It is quite common for me to meet with a client and have them ask me, "So, what are the next steps in making this happen?" I might respond this way: "I'm going to draft a brief scope of work based on our conversation and get your feedback on it. Once the scope of work is confirmed, I'll structure a budget and put together a more formal proposal for your consideration. If you have a contract that you use for external contractors, perhaps you could get me a copy of that to review. How does that sound?"

- If the scope of work is already written and well articulated, it may be appropriate to discuss any budget limitations the client has and your hourly/daily rate. Do not estimate what the job will cost until you've got the scope of work on paper and you've done a first analysis of the budget.

If at all possible, you should never make a client wait on a scope of work. Clients want to feel as though their project is a priority, and you will find no better way to show this than by writing, editing, and sending a scope of work by the end of business that day or by close of eyes that night. You want them to have it first thing the next day. Do not rush so much that you make errors in the submission. Go the extra mile to ensure that the document is accurate with no spelling or grammatical errors and that all names, titles, and company titles are correct. If you're a lousy writer, now is the time to start identifying your professional editors.

One final point of advice: Never work without a contract. Don't do it, ever, unless you've agreed to work pro bono. If your potential client is not able to move a contract through for you in a timely way, they may never produce one. At times, you may invest some business development time and go back and forth on the scope of work, but at some point, you have to draw a line: Any ongoing refinement should be billable hours.

Payment Structure

As noted above, agreeing to a payment structure is a key element of any contract. In my experience, different structures have their advantages and disadvantages.

Hourly or Daily

Some consultants meticulously track their work hours. Generally, I'm not one of them, but some clients have required hourly documentation for our contracts. In these cases, I have always used a simple Excel spreadsheet with a line for each day of the month and a pull-down list for all projects and time investments (including volunteer, business development, and personal time). This tracking system has helped me analyze my productivity. More importantly, at the end of a month, I have a simple way to see how much I need to bill each client. This approach is incredibly efficient if you have more than one client but you're not at the level of complexity where you need time tracking for multiple people. Keep in mind that if you have a business that provides services to government entities, having a formal time-tracking system is essential.

Of course, time-tracking programs are available for smartphones and even in QuickBooks and other invoice-creating programs; however, I'm trying to teach you the do-it-simple-and-do-it-cheap approach. A spreadsheet continues to be my favorite way of tracking hours. I did not start out tracking hours on all of my projects, and I regret that negligence. Hourly time tracking is incredibly important if you want to look back and determine whether your budget for a particular project ended up being spot-on. As a new consultant, I simply worked hard enough to deliver all that I agreed to deliver, regardless of whether I was losing money, by investing the extra time. This guaranteed delivery is part of what it means to be a contractor. However, if I had recorded and assessed my time expenditures, I would have been able to better plan for later projects. So, I highly recommend tracking your hours. You can also download an excellent time-tracking resource on my website, http://www.createtheworkyouwant.com/.

Each budget you craft for a particular project with a new client entails trial and error. Over time, you will get better at determining how much time different tasks take and estimating your costs. Some projects will be a wildcard and simply take longer than you could have anticipated. Ideally, every project budget will have some extra room built in, so that you can land in about the right place on your time and cost estimates.

You can build an entire budget based on hour estimates—fleshing out what you think each task will take and how much you will charge by the hour. Most clients don't want to enter into an hourly engagement with someone without a sense of how much it's going to cost to get the work done. If it's a particularly long engagement, then you can phase the work: Part one will include these services for X hours with X deliverable, and part two will include these services for X hours, etc. Your proposal should include deliverables and date estimates. The benefit of this approach is that if part one begins to include many more hours than anticipated, you may have a chance to revisit the SOW (statement of work) with the client sooner rather than later.

You can also structure a budget based on days of time. Day estimates are less granular than hourly estimates, and they give you some flexibility. For example, I know it will take me several hours to edit a report that is 60 pages long, so I might put one day in the budget for editing and review. It does not have to be a precise estimate of time. Again, you can present the work in phases, then keep track of your time so that you can assess how close to your estimate you were in the end. You could renegotiate later phases based on how time got spent in the first phase and what remains in the client's budget.

Fixed Cost

If a client is willing to think beyond hourly and daily billing, larger project-oriented contracts can be arranged through a fixed-cost approach. This type is always preferred for a consultant because it's much more predictable. It is also a more predictable cost for the client, so in contract negotiations, remind everyone of the mutual benefit. Most of the work that I do with clients is set up this way. Estimating an accurate project price requires that you have a fairly solid sense of the time it takes to do tasks and the time it takes to coordinate work with a particular company or organization. If you do a poor job estimating the work and it takes you more time and resources, you usually have to eat the costs; so build in some padding on your time estimates. On the positive side, in some cases you will be so efficient with your time and resources that you underspend, leading to unexpected extra money.

As a consultant in design and communications, Colin strongly prefers fixed-cost contracts. He has found that it is hard to get paid well if you charge per hour. Clients may balk at paying him $300 per hour, but they may agree to paying $3,000 for the entire project (which he can complete in 10 hours). Because of Colin's experience and efficiency, he knows what his time is worth. Using a fixed-cost payment structure has worked for him and for his clients.

Keep in mind a few key items about fixed-cost projects. If they are multiyear, you should add in an adjustment for annual cost-of-living increases. It is not reasonable that you or anybody who works for you will be paid the same amount year after year. It is also important that you still keep track of your spending. Just because a client pays you a stated amount for a scope of work doesn't mean you stop tracking your output. You have to be able to look back over time and see if you estimated well. This is crucial data for creating more accurate budgets. Because my company does a great deal of data collection, we have a clear handle on what site visits cost on average, what transcription fees are for individual and group interviews, and how much time it takes to analyze this kind of data. I also have a host of subcontractors whose work and fees I know. If you're going to be pricing out projects, accumulating this kind of information is helpful.

In some very rare instances—if and only if I believe *client* factors have contributed to the overrun in budget or time—I've gone back to clients to discuss issues with the scope of work and ask for a budget revision. I renegotiate only if I have a strong and established relationship with the client and when my arguments for the overages are quite clear. Obviously, such a conversation is not optimal and can be best avoided by preparing detailed starting budgets and tracking task hours over time.

Retainers

Retainers are another approach to contracts, where a client pays an amount of money up front to secure your services. The retainer structure is often music to a contractor's ears. Retainers are useful when the scope of work is highly undefined. For example, say a client wants assistance doing internal work such as training and development, strategic planning, or quality control around some not-fully-defined needs. Such internal demands often require several meetings and much creativity; the processes are iterative, and the path forward is not clear until you have dug in. So if the client has agreed to pay you a certain amount for your time each month, you have plenty of flexibility to accommodate their needs.

That said, a retainer still requires a defined scope of work. These questions can help shape your work plans:

- What are the client's goals for the retainer relationship?
- In what area would the client like to make progress or improvements?
- What does the client want to achieve by the end of the period you've worked together?

Once you've articulated this set of statements, review and revise them until they reflect your and your client's expectations. Now you have something to reference for periodic evaluation. You might consider scheduling a biweekly or monthly call, depending on the length and intensity of the contract, to discuss the clients' perceptions of progress on the established scope of work. After these calls, summarize what you heard and directions for the next period; share that summary with the client to ensure that both of you are on the same page.

Working with a retainer is my absolute favorite approach because you still have to estimate the budget and track your time, but you can now rely on a fixed amount of money on a steady basis. Some clients like retainer contracts because they know you'll be billing a consistent amount each month and they can rely on having your attention for a specified number of days per week.

You can also structure your week so that you're focusing on a particular project for specific days. In some cases, I have actually gone to the office of a retainer client for one or two days a week, logging the majority of my time face-to-face with them on those days. Being physically present has been a wonderful way to get to know a company inside and out, as it provides the opportunity for conversations with all personnel.

Getting Paid

Whatever your approach to the payment structure with a new client, think about how you would like to be paid. Payment terms are stipulated in virtually every contract, and clients vary in their approaches. Timing matters. If you're planning to use subcontractors, they will want to be paid on time. You don't want to be left cash poor while you're paying everyone else and awaiting your client's 30-45 days payment turnaround (sometimes longer if you're doing government work). In the exceptional case, such as with big government contracts, you can be paid for time and materials expended only after the fact. In all other cases, you should be asking for some amount of money up front in a negotiated budget.

Requesting money up front sounds like a tough thing to do, but it is quite common to negotiate some retainer upon the launch of a contract. One client actually agreed to pay the entirety of a project at the start of each year, for a period of four years. I wish I could say that this payment plan was my idea, but it arose from the attorney I retained to help me negotiate the contract. The up-front payment was a lifesaver on a project that required endless travel expenses and subcontractor costs.

In my contracts, I use one of four approaches to getting paid:

- Ask for 10-20% of the budget for the given year up front upon signature, then divide remaining payments, reserving 5-10% for the end of your contract.
- Ask for 25% of the budget up front; when those 25% hours are almost expended, bill for the next 25%, and so forth.
- Tie payments to service and deliverable completion points. Clients typically like this arrangement because they feel as if they're paying after you've provided what is in the agreement. As a consultant, I have not always liked this approach because I've run into scenarios where clients drag review periods out for an unfair amount of time, long after the work has transpired and my subcontractors have been paid. In those cases, it is reasonable to bill for the delays, though it won't leave a good taste in the mouth of the client. Instead, you can tie payments to the date of first draft deliverable (not completed drafts).
- Tie payments to calendar dates. This is the right approach if the deliverable dates are not controlled by you. Let's say you have to interview people, but you can't control their availability.

Your particular field may have common practices, so research payment terms and approaches. I want to highlight a few caution areas:

- *Working for one client.* Avoid having only one client. Every field has a big fish—a renowned client that will make you feel as though you've arrived in your professional world. Such big fish typically have plenty of resources to throw around, and if you do good work, they will want to control more and more of your time. But be cautious about building your business around one client. That monopoly won't go well for you in the end. Diversity is central to your long-term success.
- *Changes in staffing.* All professional settings are characterized by regular staffing and leadership changes. If a notable change happens mid-contract, carefully review any contracted work with new people in person or by phone. Clarify whether any change in the scope of work will occur and learn about any goals under new leadership.
- *Government contracts.* Depending on your field of work, professional rates may be fixed. In some cases, states have set rates for different levels of professional training and experience, and they can't stipulate a higher rate on any contract. In other cases, the company you're working with wants to hire you for a project funded by federal or state monies. They may ask you to document your income before they can agree to a contract. Learn about these expectations prior to negotiating with a client.

Managing Cash Flow

One of the trickiest dynamics of self-employment is managing cash flow. If managing budgets and cash is something at which you excel, then you may have this aspect in the bag; but for me, it was an ongoing challenge. Keep in mind that most companies you are serving are flush with cash and have far more flexibility than you as a solo contractor. You do not always have the ability to manage 30-, 45-, or 60-day payment terms.

Find out how the client typically manages consultant payments, then work out a plan that is acceptable to you. Generally speaking, companies have a financial person who cuts checks on set days of the month. If possible, contact that person to find out key details:

- Does the company offer ACH as an option for contractors? More frequently than not, this electronic funds-transfer is possible. Lock that agreement down up front so that you can be paid quickly.
- If ACH is not an option, find out when contractor checks are cut and plan to send your monthly or occasional invoices the week prior to that processing date.
- Make sure payment procedures are specified in your contract: Who receives invoices? Who needs to approve? Who needs to be copied on the invoice? When will it be paid?

A number of excellent resources are available for simple invoicing. When you first start out, you can create a simple invoice of your own or find a template on the internet. Just make sure that it includes following details: name for payment, address for payment, contact name/phone numbers, consulting activities, date period for those activities, and charges. Check out some resources on my website, http://www.createtheworkyouwant.com/.

For almost all of my consulting years, I have used QuickBooks online. One of its helpful features is that you can see when the invoice was received, opened, and viewed. The invoices are customizable, and if you're tracking expenses in QuickBooks, you now have all your financials in one place. In addition to QuickBooks, a number of other resources exist in this space for a range of costs (e.g. FreshBooks, Square, Hiveage).

Summary

- When possible, discuss contracts in person or over the phone, covering all relevant points.
- Know the advantages and disadvantages of hourly, daily, fixed-cost, and stipend payment structures.
- Make sure that contracts include payment terms that provide the cash flow you need.
- Send detailed invoices shortly before a company's bills are paid each month.

Being an Extraordinary Professional

I would not have fully done my job with this book if I didn't devote one short section to professionalism as a self-employed business or service provider. After many years of doing business, I have realized that the following points are not common knowledge.

Common Sense Professionalism

Making professional choices and acting in professional ways is key to developing your reputation as a business. The following practices have contributed to the success of my company:

- Don't pretend you know something when you don't. Being a solo contractor doesn't mean you're the expert at everything. Instead, you are a person who can join a team to help them accomplish goals. You can learn (on your own time) and hire people to help you accomplish something with the resources you have at your disposal.

- Be on time for all meetings, whether they are by phone or in person. If you're using meeting software, get familiar with it before the call so you're able to join in immediately and respect the time of your clients. If you are meeting in person, try to learn in advance about parking recommendations, security and entrances, suite numbers, and meeting rooms. You want your client to feel that working with you is effortless.

- If you as a contractor are working with senior-level people, which is often the case, find out if they have a scheduler or administrative assistance. Many senior people do not book their own meetings and don't want to be involved with this level of detail. You are a guest to the companies and organizations that you serve, and you have to engage in a way that is very easy for the client. In general, work within the culture of each company.

- Know the company dress codes, and if you don't yet have that information, err on the side of dressing up. Few companies today are suited up in formal work attire, but some are still out there. Even if a company you serve has employees wearing jeans to work, I would never recommend arriving in jeans. You can maintain a well-dressed casual appearance with a simple pair of dress casual pants or skirts. Some organizations might be more on the creative side where people dress with more flair, accentuate with more color, jewelry, and bold hairstyles. While you represent your own company, you also need to portray an image and style that others will find easy to invite and fit into their company culture.

- Don't waste clients' time. If you're invited to a meeting, and no one is clearly in charge of the meeting, then you should suggest an agenda. Simply indicate that you want to establish goals for the meeting, and ask others if they have agenda items to add for the agreed-upon time frame. Devote time in advance to thinking through meetings. These are valuable real estate in your client's day and yours. Figure out in advance what needs to get accomplished, what you need to learn and know in that meeting, and what might be next steps following the meeting. In an initial meeting with a client that is more in the genre of business development, an agenda may not be appropriate. But for your own sake, thinking in advance about the meeting's objectives will be worthwhile. My most important reminder about meetings is that before they end, everyone should agree on next steps and a time frame for accomplishing them.

- Follow up the meeting with an email articulating a high level summary, including any agreements that were made and next steps that were planned with dates and names of responsible parties. If during a meeting, decisions are made that impact anything in a scope of work that you're contracted to do, be sure to also follow up with a separate message to the contract signer, articulating the change that was made to the contract plan.

- Do your best to spell-check and reread anything that you send to a client to avoid grammatical and typographical errors. Mistakes happen, and they aren't the end of the world, but slow down and reduce the errors in your communication. Typos, especially, convey sloppiness that will impact the way people view your work.

Giving Back with Your Business

We all launch our own businesses to make a living and to be happier with our own life choices. But once you are on your feet and experiencing success, think about how you are going to give back with your business. How is your business going to make the world a better place?

When I began my company, this question was the furthest from my mind. But as I moved forward, I realized that I didn't want to think solely of myself—I wanted to focus on more than just me. I took a couple different approaches to giving. Since I worked in the world of higher education policy, a simple, no-brainer way to make a difference was to contribute to organizations that were doing good work in the areas of my passions. I made annual donations to nonprofit college access organizations and programs that supported low-income students. I also channeled some of my alumni gifts toward scholarship programs and supports for underrepresented populations in higher education.

Perhaps even more importantly than giving money, I used the perspective that I had on the field to meet with younger professionals and offer advice, a listening ear, and connections where I could. As you become a person who is senior in your profession, you can offer up social/professional capital for others in your field, especially those who are lacking the right connections. This is also a good time to offer some of your expertise pro bono. For example, I have offered one-to-one counseling support for older adults trying to navigate the pathway to higher education. I have also offered my services for free (or at reduced cost) to fledging organizations that need my services but can't afford to fully pay for them. It has also been my privilege to serve on community boards, as well as school boards.

Working in strategic planning and advancement in higher education, Ellen travels a lot. But when she is at her home base in Arizona, she volunteers with the Be a Leader Foundation in Phoenix. As a Senior Boot Camp Coach, she works with high school mentees who are applying for college. Not only does she enjoy this venue for giving back, but her involvement also educates her about her community and functions as a form of professional development. As a result of her volunteer role, she has become more aware and knowledgeable about what is happening at the ground level, and will be working with the executive team of the organization on strategic planning.

If you choose to give of yourself on occasion and with intention, your life and the lives of others will be enriched. Extraordinary professionals give back.

Asking for Input

When I was trying to launch my business, I knew that I needed help. I heard about a business coach through a friend and decided to give her a try. We sat down for a consultation lunch to get to know each other and to see if we were a good match. After a lot of back and forth where I explained my strange career trajectory, she asked me what it was that I loved about my work. I paused for a second and looked away to gather my thoughts ... then said that I love using my research skills to help organizations learn. She asked me if I had any colleagues from my previous jobs who could attest to my skill in this arena. In fact I did: I told her that I had previously been employed by a company that I loved, where a key person was now the president of a company in my field. At this point she stopped me and said, "Well, that is just amazing! How fortunate. Have you spoken with this person about your new business and your passion for this work?" As you can imagine, the answer was no. My reason? I was afraid. I was so busy talking about and planning the work I was going to do that I hadn't taken much action to actually *do* anything.

Right there in the middle of a noisy D.C. lunch crowd, this coach whom I had not yet hired had me role-play that phone call right over our salads. It was awkward and slightly embarrassing. But onward we went. And after we rehearsed the script a few times, where I tell this major potential advocate about my new business plans, she reminded me to pause and ask the central question: "So, what do you think of all that?" (Or stated another way: "I would love your thoughts/feedback on what I've shared.")

This conversation was profoundly important because many of us will go around yapping our faces off to people (sometimes out of insecurity, sometimes to appear more confident than we are, sometimes because we think we know it all). We rarely pause to ask for input, and even more rarely take the risk of asking for someone's help. We resist being vulnerable. It is risky as we might hear something that doesn't encourage us on our path. But we just might get the kind of input and help that sets our lives on a new course. This was a lesson that I've taken to heart for all the days of my business life. Still today, I regularly take opportunities to ask friends, clients, colleagues, and family for input on the things

I'm doing, pondering, creating, and struggling with—and I try to stay open and curious toward their input.

Eventually I did call that company president and had a fruitful discussion about the business I was seeking to build. Over the course of several months, that call ended up leading to a business contract and a long-time client relationship—one that brought over $1 million in revenues to my business.

Trusting Your Intuition

When I first began the journey of self-employment, I wasn't sure that I wanted to work for myself. Even though I was regularly providing consulting services doing research, data analysis, and publication development late in my graduate program, I continued to go on job interviews. A few times, I went quite far with the interview process, but each time something just didn't feel right. The bottom line was that I enjoyed my freedom. I had two small children, and I was seriously involved in a master's rowing program, a time-intensive hobby with training and races. Each time I went on a job interview, it seemed like people wanted to hire me for positions that paid less than what I was garnering on an hourly basis doing research as a graduate student. I had three interviews where the salary discussions were not enticing, particularly as I considered the commute, the 9-5 hours, and the inflexible travel schedule.

Oddly enough, the turning point for me committing to working for myself was not getting a new client but leaving an old one. I had been consistently working for a large nonprofit producing an annual data publication. It was a big project, and for a part of the year I was able to bill close to full-time hours. However, because the publication had a fair amount of notoriety in my field, most people assumed that I worked only for that company. This scenario leads to another one of my great lessons—trusting your gut.

I had this sense that the path forward was to bump up my hourly rate with the client to move it from grad school pay to real pay *or* to move on from that organization in search of clients who wanted a professional with my skills. Being a huge extrovert, I have this habit of trying out my thoughts and ideas on my 10 closest friends. This method is risky. On the plus side, talking through my idea moves my thinking forward. But when you invite others into that "thinking," you are bound to find some naysayers. One of my dear friends at that time thought the idea of leaving my current paying gig to launch my own business was completely insane. In truth, the thought of giving up the security scared me too, but I still wanted to take the risk. The deal was sealed when the response to the pay bump was an outright no, so onward I went.

Final Thoughts

This book was designed to help you launch your business. Nothing that I tell you can provide enough assurance. It has to come from you. Your sense of right timing needs to be trusted. You ultimately have to believe with some amount of certainty that your capabilities are the asset upon which you want to build your business, and that creating the work you want is the right path for you.

I've provided here what I've absorbed through years of trying to get this right. I'll probably save you from making some errors, but I promise that you will still make plenty of your own. I would have liked to live no other way than working for myself all of these years. Perhaps I'll change my path one day in the future, but for now, I want to be the creator of my day, my week, my months, and my life. Working for myself has made it possible for me to travel on a whim, to spend entire summers at the beach with my kids, and to allow my energy and passion for work drive what I elect to do and who I elect to work with on a project. Sure, I have moments of disappointment, and some of the work I've chosen feels hard some days, but each of those moments have been learning opportunities for how to do it better—how to craft a business that I want to wake up to and succeed at each and every day.

Manufactured by Amazon.ca
Bolton, ON

34457912R00072